Experiment in Architecture

Frank Stepper, Timo Carl,
Sarah Blahut (Eds.)

Experiment in Architecture

Thinking the Unthinkable and Realizing the Impossible

Birkhäuser
Basel

Frank Stepper's Journey Through Architecture

By Hitoshi Abe

I first met Frank Stepper in the 1980s when I was a student in the Coop Himmelb(l)au (CHBL) studio at the Southern California Institute of Architecture in Santa Monica. A man with long, shaggy hair, distinctive round glasses, and a leather jacket slung over his shoulder quietly entered the studio behind the instructor, Wolf Prix, with a smile on his face. He had moved to Los Angeles from Southern Germany to preside over the newly established CHBL Los Angeles office for the planned Open House project in Malibu, and to teach the SCI-ARC studio. This was the beginning of a long relationship with Frank, first as his student, then as his staff member at CHBL, and then as his friend to this day.

At that time, CHBL-LA had a number of experimental projects underway, including Open House and the Osaka Exposition Follies. I spent my days learning from him as we worked together in an environment where we were challenged to fundamentally reexamine the basic framework of architecture and push the bounds of what is considered possible. Frank, who drives a disproportionately large 1970s classic American car and serves German food with his culinary skills, is essentially a traveler by nature. No matter how many years had passed since he moved to L.A., no matter how familiar he was with the L.A. context, he always seemed to be an outsider. As a fellow traveler from Japan who had not yet been to Europe, I was exposed to a European culture and way of thinking that was foreign to me. Travel is the act of temporarily leaving one's place of residence and going to another, and the immersion in a new environment causes one to review the environment that supports and shapes them in their daily life. In the old days, the word "journey" did not necessarily refer to going to a distant land, but to leaving one's residence. By standing on the common ground of Los Angeles with a traveler from another place, I was able to move back and forth between the three cultural spheres of Japan, Los Angeles, and Germany on a daily basis without ever leaving my city. I believe this has taught me to question, reevaluate, and redefine the everyday aspects of my own life.

Architecture refers to both the act that results in the production a structure and the structure itself. It is both the product and the technology that produces it. If this is the case, then the evolution of architecture that many of us are pursuing is driven by innovations in these two aspects, innovations in "the people who perform the act of designing building" or "the technology that produces the building." The keyword, "travel" in Frank Stepper's work seems to correspond to this "human," and "innovation in the technology that produces buildings." Needless to say, "travel" changes people. The view of the 405 Freeway filled with an unbelievable number of cars in Los Angeles, the beautiful and overcrowded convenience stores in Tokyo, the ad-hoc rooftop constructions in Taipei, the bustling souks in Istanbul, the people resting in New York's Central Park—these elements unique to each place have an undeniable effect on those that inhabit them. By leaving the background that shapes one's life and immersing oneself in the customs, cultures, and cities of different places, one can merge their own experience with that of a foreign land to create a new background. With each journey, the background that shapes the subject is transformed. For architects who are in charge of the design of people's lives and their vessels, it is an important opportunity to externalize oneself and objectively view their relationship to the world. This in turn expands possibilities for innovation by changing the one performing the act of architecture, which will undeniably influence its outcome. I believe this is the reason travel has been associated with architects since the ancient times.

When discussing architecture with Frank, I sometimes feel like he is a bit of a mad scientist. In fictional works, it is the mad scientist who deviates from the established framework of the world, conducting unapologetically ambitious experiments that may scare or confuse people. We often talked about his ideas to diverge from architectural conventions and open up new possibilities. Perhaps it was his demeanor and the grin he wore when discussing interesting ideas that gave me this impression, or it may have been his experimental approach to the architectural design process. Experimentation means testing and examining the validity of a hypothesis, especially in the natural sciences where artificial conditions that cause phenomena to occur are set up in order to study, observe, and measure their outcomes. Our process at that time was not the usual deductive approach to design, but rather one in which we dared to create a phenomenon by applying certain conditions to a ready-made architectural framework. This process, carried out mainly through models while incorporating happenings that occur along the way, ultimately proves how to realize the seemingly unrealizable hypothetical structures and spaces that arise by making full use of various technologies. The act of creating the impossible through experimentation and realizing it through proof in the design process can truly be called a "journey of technology to create architecture."

In experimentation, matter changes its characteristics as it is placed in new contexts, just like a person traveling on a journey. The geometry of countless nails collected by magnets, the curves of dripping liquid, the trajectory of exploding balloons: these events become new conditions that overlap with the architectural process to give it new frameworks, transform old ones, and lead to the technological innovations that make the ideas possible. For Frank Stepper, experimentation with architecture is a journey.

This book is a compilation of the many journeys taken by Frank Stepper and his students. By sending architecture to distant horizons, he is opening up new possibilities.

Entering the Universe of Possibilities

by Marie-Therese Harnoncourt-Fuchs

Entering the Universe of Possibilities

By Marie-Therese Harnoncourt-Fuchs

The endless possibilities of thinking about and arranging space into an ever-changing social discourse is why I am an architect. The introductory project in the first year of the BA course at the University of Kassel enters into this universe of possibilities and intends to capture the interest of the students. The desire and curiosity to discover are essential prerequisites for developing a forward-looking position and language in architecture. In my thinking, there is no such thing as ideal architecture, but architecture that touches and challenges, and I primarily speak about the qualities and properties of spaces and their possibilities of use.

Experimental Design

Design is thinking in future scenarios. The design process is a gradual approach to a possible future reality that combines all requirements and ideas in one spatial form. It is a complex process that challenges our logical, analytical, intuitive, and creative thinking in equal measure and should therefore always be practiced as a process, and with all senses in my opinion.

For me, experimental design means getting involved in the design process. Only in this way can the possibilities that arise from the process be discovered as such and tried out impartially. This includes entering unknown territory, throwing conventional habits overboard, and being open to the unforeseen.

Just as Cosimo left his father's table in Italo Calvino's novel *The Baron in the Trees* to live in the trees and never set foot on the ground again, experimental design is also a "consciousness cure" to leave familiar paths and ideas in order to see other, often even obvious, possibilities.

"Space is a doubt: I have to constantly mark it out, designate it; it is never mine, it will never be given to me, I must conquer it." Quote from George Perec.

Creating / Challenging Spatial Concepts

Experimental design cannot merely be taught from a theoretical level. Experimental design develops through "learning by doing" and must be discovered by everyone with all of their senses. How to start and develop the design process, and what parameters the design is based on, is hence an essential part of my architecture teaching. There are tools and methods, but no recipes. The design process requires a personal approach, which the students should find and develop for themselves as part of their studies. The interweaving of the physical and digital worlds has created an extremely productive terrain, a new territory in working with complex spatial concepts and structures. I encourage working "with all means," with algorithms and straws, with analogue, digital, and digitally fabricated models, with images, films, sounds, and language. That is why, in teaching design, students should learn how to test and mediate using a wide variety of tools and methods. Failure and success have equal potential in creative and imaginative project development.

Make Spatial Concepts Visible and Communicate Them

We work passionately with working models that are quick to build and easy to change to support the work and thought process more effectively. In my opinion, the true-to-scale analogue physical model, as a haptic abstraction of a design idea, has regained importance; as in the digital design process, scales are difficult for students to grasp. The current developments via AR / VR, allowing 1:1 access and entry into digital models, is however, a new and extremely exciting possibility. We are in the process of examining them in teaching and research for their potential for the design process and the presentation of spatial concepts. For me, it is not about either or, but rather about exploiting and promoting the potential of the interrelationships between digital and analogue tools. Architecture is a medium that is communicated on different levels. It is therefore natural to work on projects conceptually in analogue and digital form, both in the design process and in the project presentation.

The Experiment at EEK

For Frank, the introductory project was always a special concern, and his experimental design theory has shaped entire generations. There was no fear of the first line. It started with experiments on a scale of 1:1. Depending on the task, whether cast, melted, folded, cut, generated, added... the processes and the resulting structures were observed... their spatial and structural properties and qualities were analyzed in order to derive a spatial principle for the further design. In this way, the students were involved in complex spatial structures without realizing it. The models were photographed, measured, drawn, digitized, and transformed. At the final exhibition as part of the ASL (University of Kassel's Institute for Architecture, Urban and Landscape Planning) tour, eek's introductory studio was immediately recognizable by its "space-telling" sectional drawings, its large-scale cardboard models, and the derivation of the experimental design process with model studies, photos, and / or small film sequences.

Freethinking

Experimentation with space; letting oneself drift in the possibilities that open up in the course of the work process, taking the seemingly secondary, not architecturally adequate (whatever that might be?) seriously, discovering one's own passions... is a formative experience that requires a lot of time, work, and an unconditional commitment... and is a first immersion in this universe of possibilities of space / architecture.

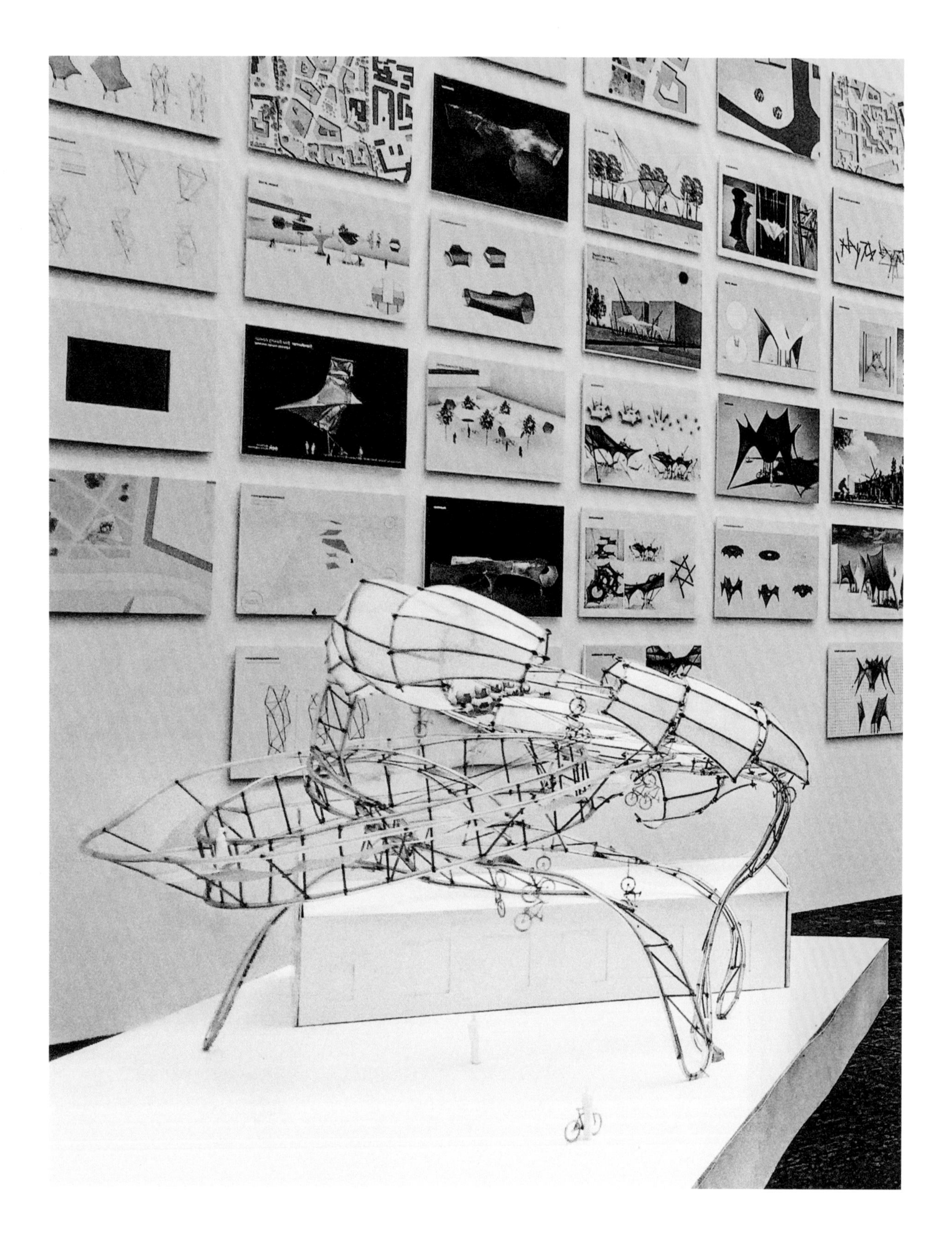

Radhäuser

The "radHAUS" (bikeHOUSE) project provides an experimental and playful contribution to the current debate around the inclusion of bicycle as the preferred mode of transportation for contemporary urban mobility. Students explore the emerging potential for the design of novel infrastructure in the urban realm required for green modes of transport. The focus is on the "bicycle" as starting point of a pavilion architecture with transformative character that allows students to engage in the conscious generation in the "city of tomorrow".

Physical experiments that engage in the topic of movement inform first design ideas for the formulation of spatial concepts. Documented by video, the experiments revolve around aspects of time, space, magnetism, or spatial networks, thereby linking them in artistic ways to the broader topic of cycling. The interaction of digital and analogue methods underscores the dynamic of the topic and design process. The Holländischer Platz of the University of Kassel campus serves as a real world testing ground for the spatial utopias of 19 students, who envisioned multifunctional bike architectures.

The works situate themselves at the interface between architecture and art, reality and visionary spatial interventions. Plans and models of the radHAUS studio were part of the "FahrRad!" exhibition of the German Architecture Museum at the documenta-Halle in Kassel.

EXPERIMENT
↙ VIDEO

Project: Bike Carousel, 2019
by David Sadowsky, Axel Lippmann
Experiment "Centrifugal Force"

Bike Carousel, model scale 1:50

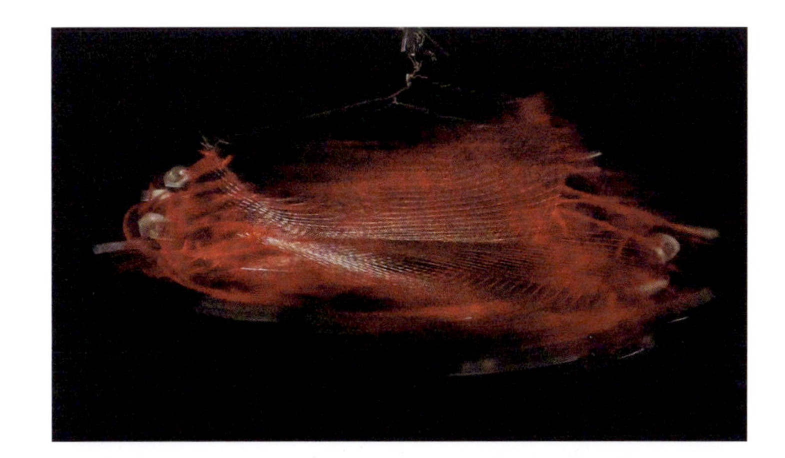

video stills from experiment

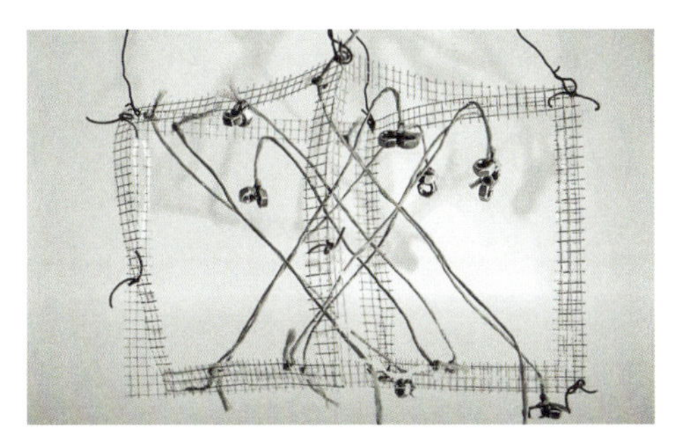

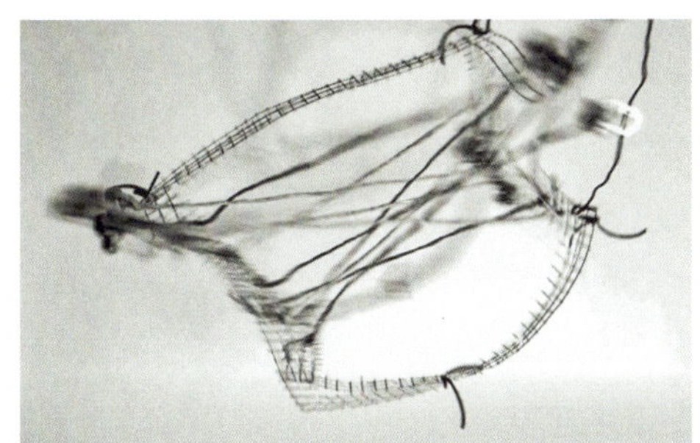

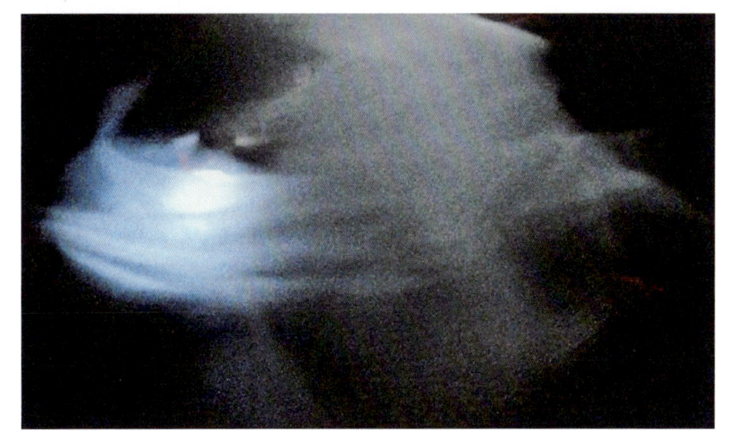

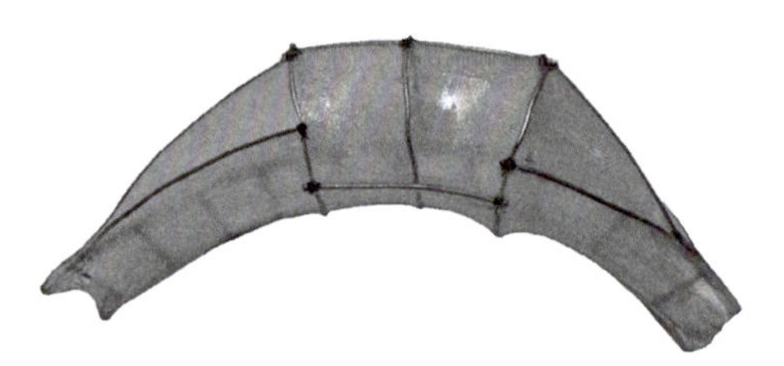

step 1: sail form-finding

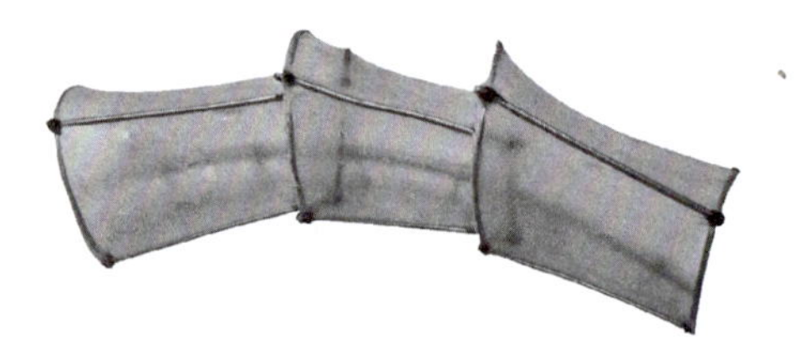

step 2: sail divided into individual modules

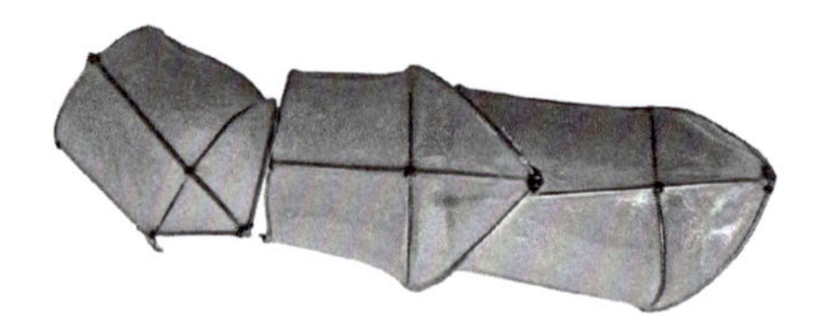

step 3: shape adjusted according to dynamic effect

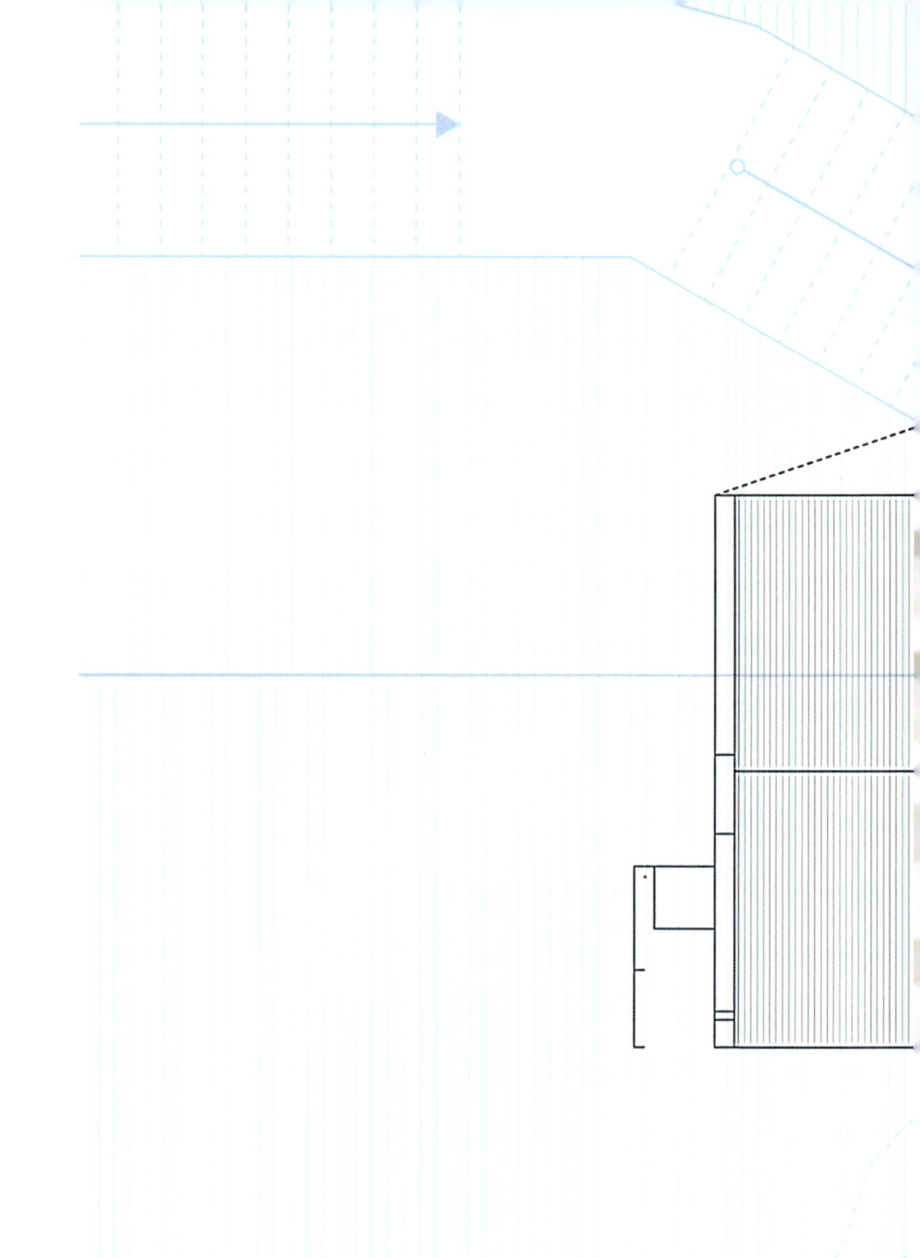

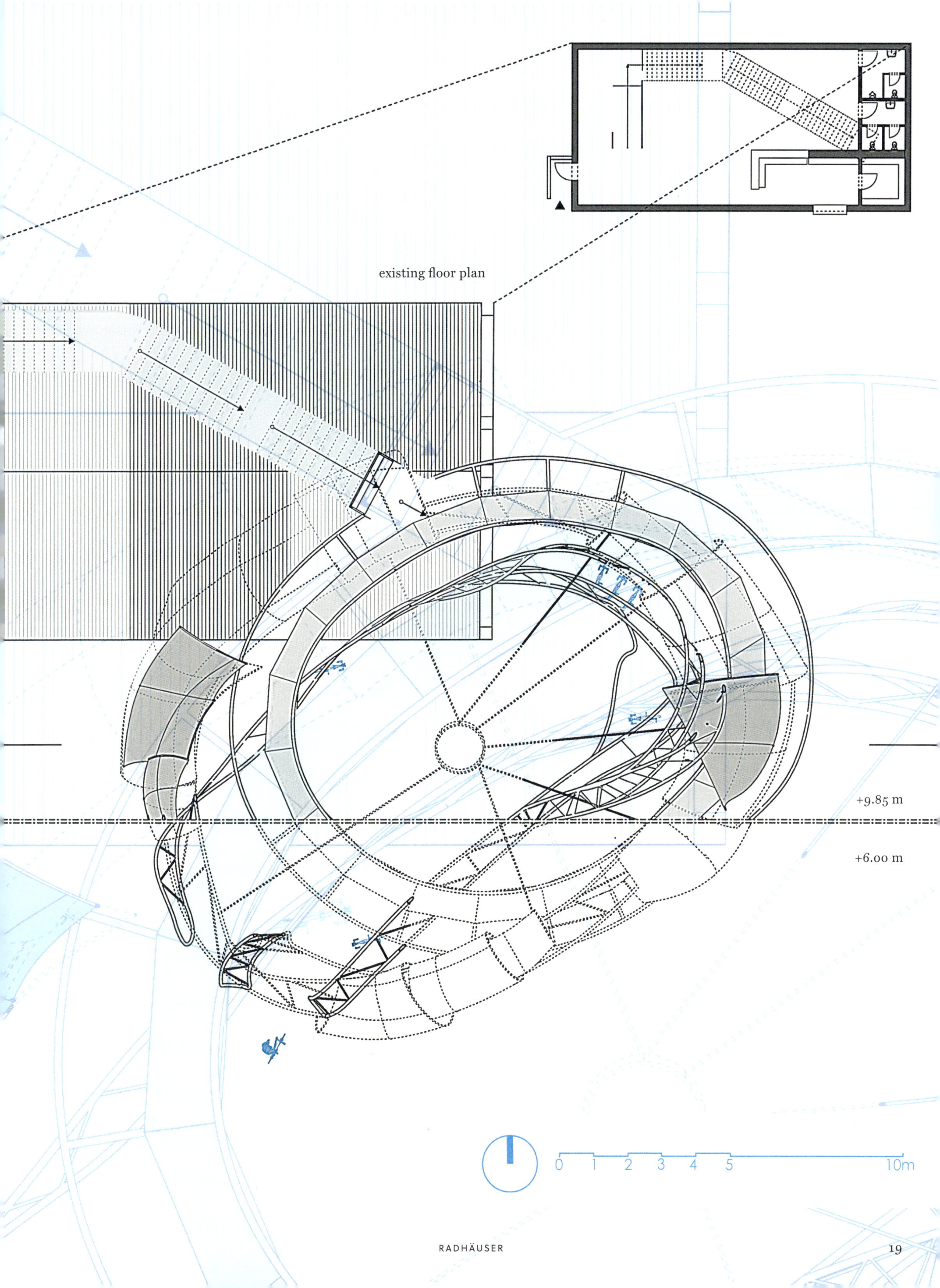
existing floor plan
+9.85 m
+6.00 m
0 1 2 3 4 5 10m

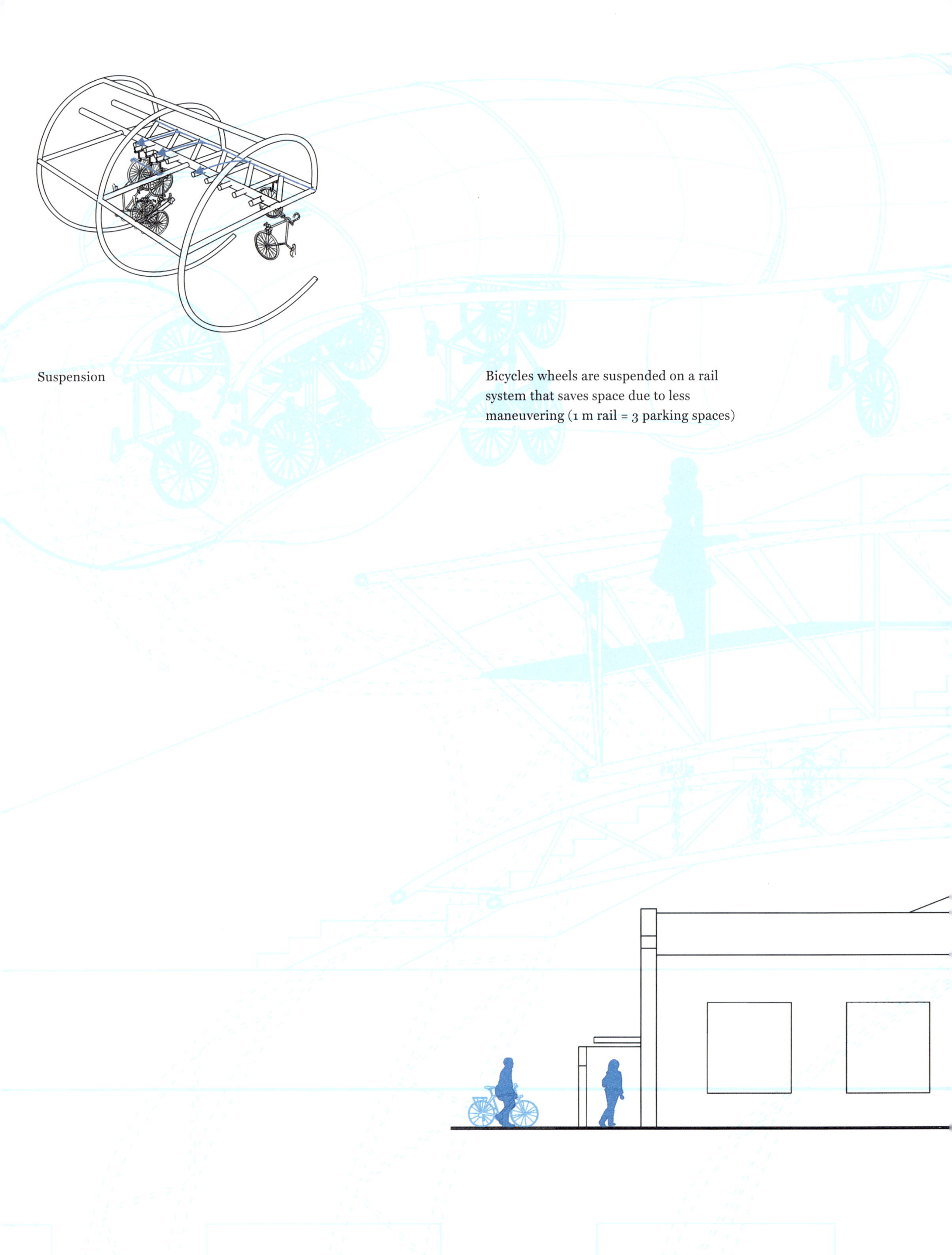

Suspension

Bicycles wheels are suspended on a rail system that saves space due to less maneuvering (1 m rail = 3 parking spaces)

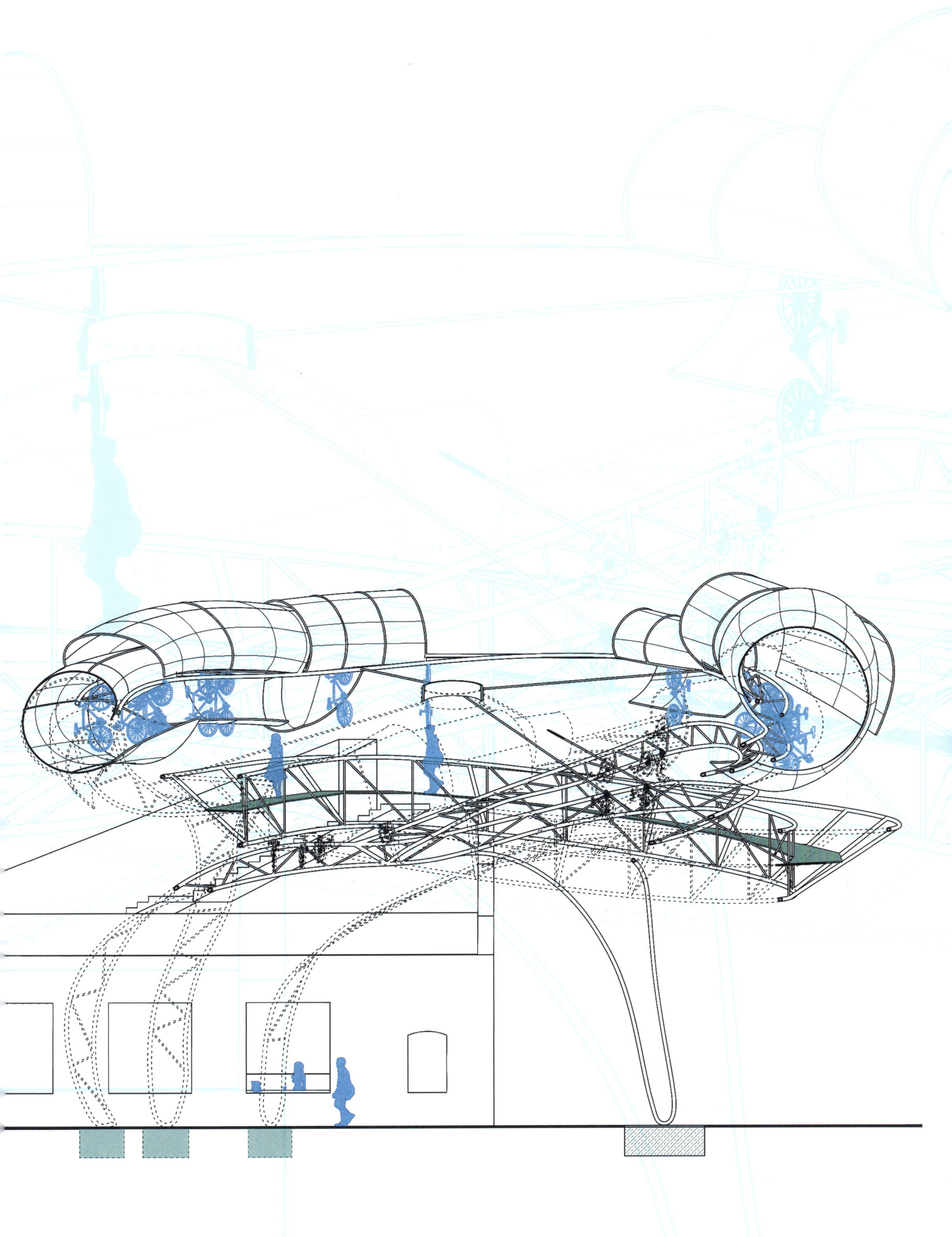

Bike Carousel, model scale 1:50

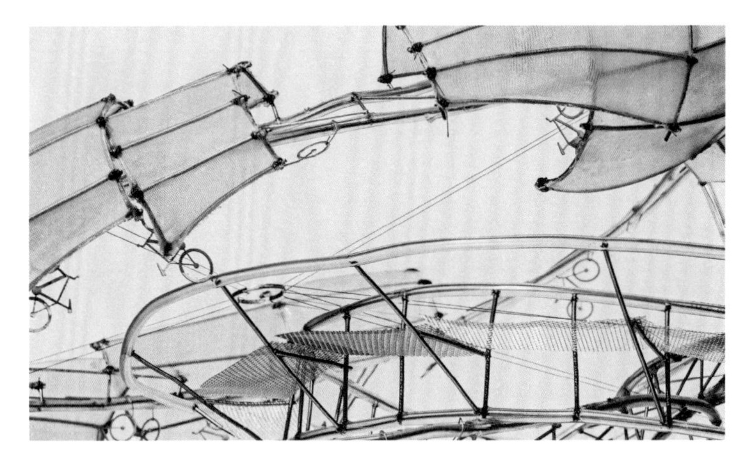

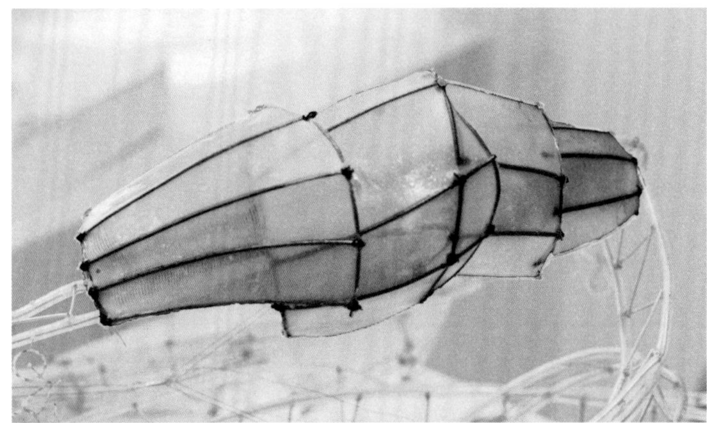

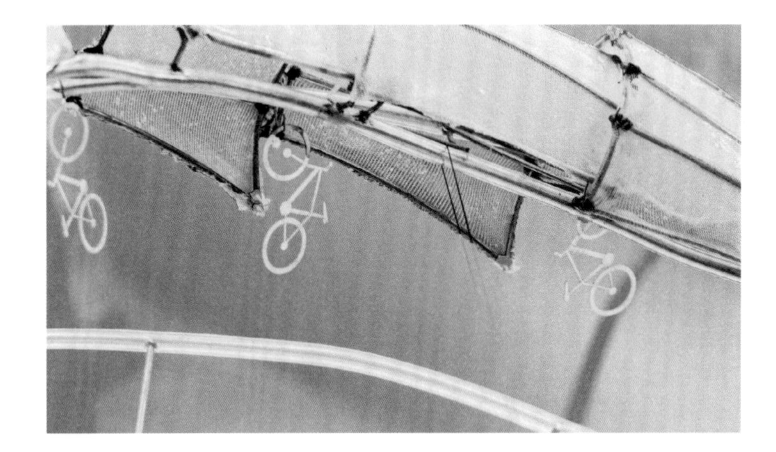

Park der (T)Räume

Park der (T)räume (Park of Dreams or Spaces). New Follies for the Champ de Mars

The notion of the Folly is an ambiguous one that is architecturally vague. As Cedric Price noted so elegantly: The folly distorts time, place, and space and in so doing mixes magic with mystery, fun with fantasy, "now" with "then".[1] Therefore, the type of the "Folly" is all the more suitable as an experimental field for the production of new spatial ideas. It fosters conceptual and creative thinking and design for the students. Eliminating the need for functional program and representative function helped students to explore and identify spatial ideas with the help of a series of physical real world experiments. Students translated and developed their "found" ideas into a series of concrete architectural artifacts for the Champ de Mars in Paris.

1 Arata Isozaki, Cedric Price, and Koji Taki, Osaka Follies (London: Architectural Association, 1991), 11.

Project: Magnetic Space, 2015
by Sarah Metwally, Eugenia Schlag
Experiment "Magnetism"

experiment in water

structure and space

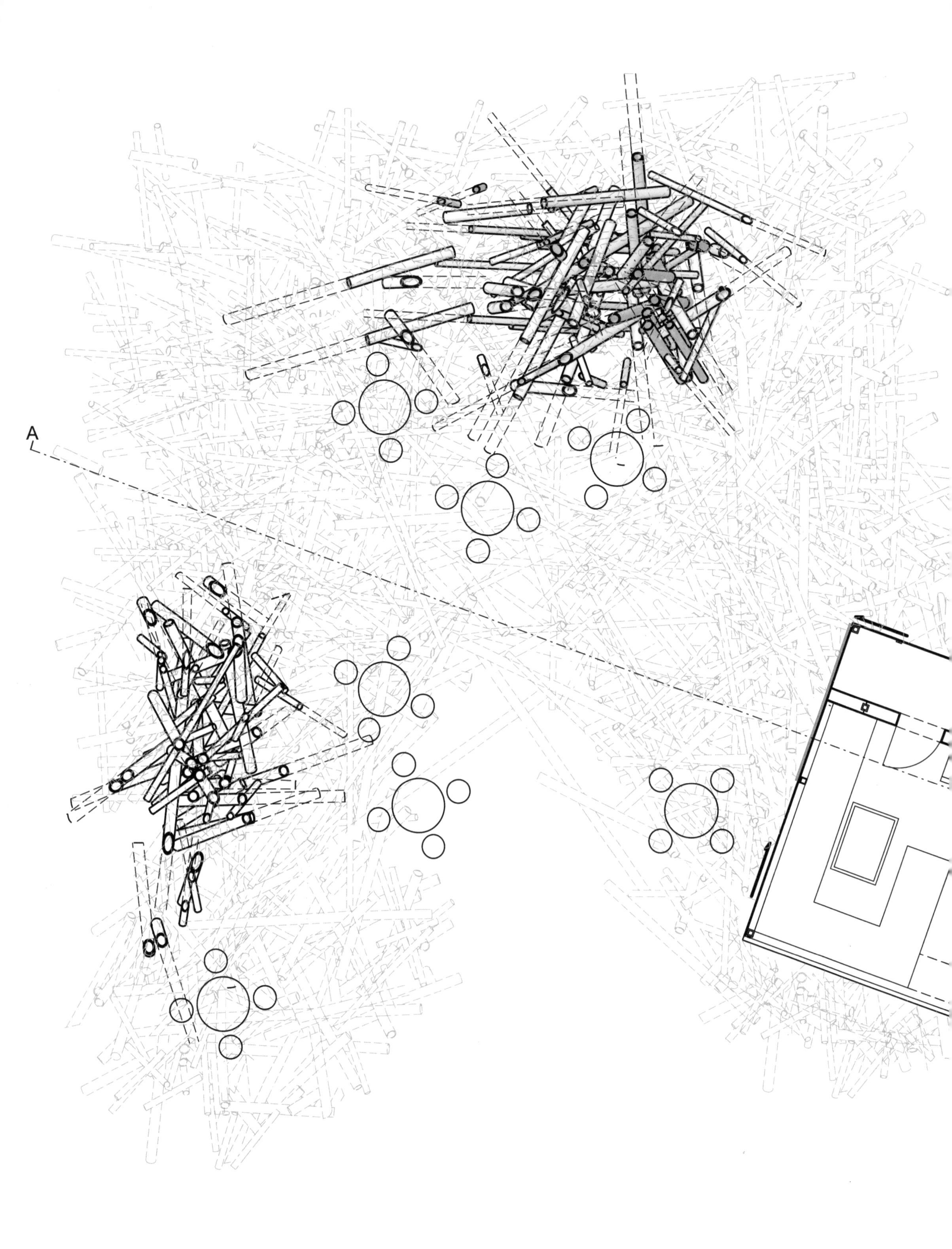
A

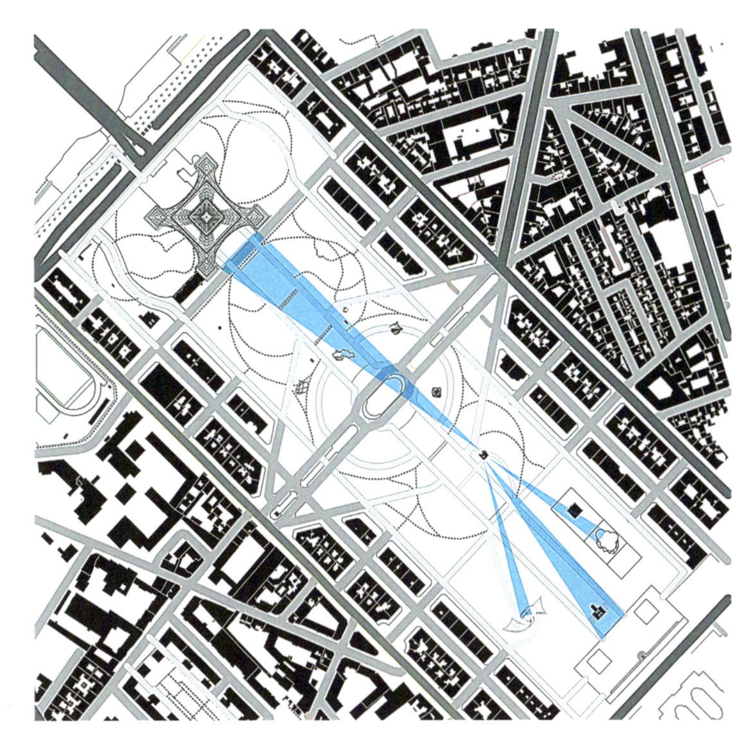

Site plan: Champs du Mars – Paris

The pavilion serves as a summer café. The cube acts as
a support for the structure as well as the enclosure of the café.

ground floor plan

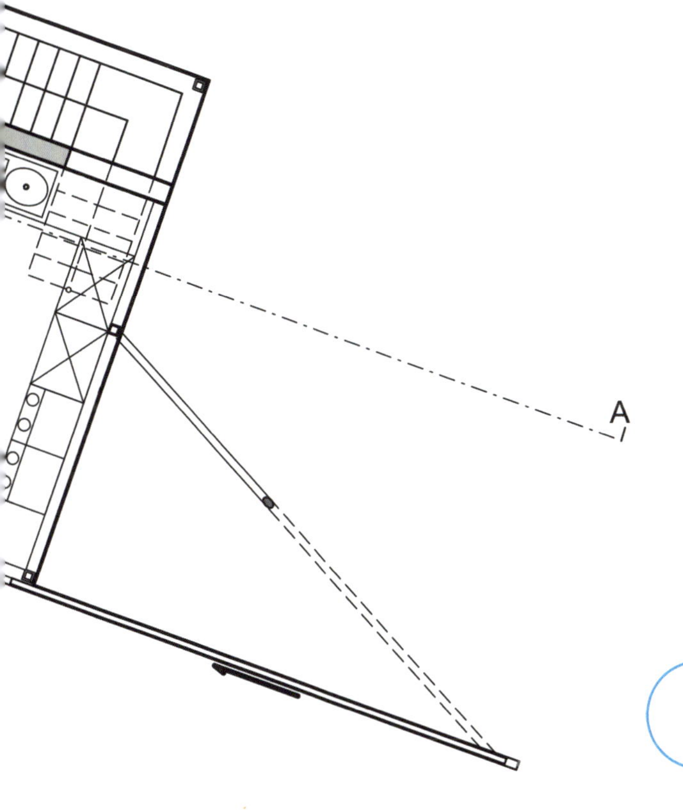

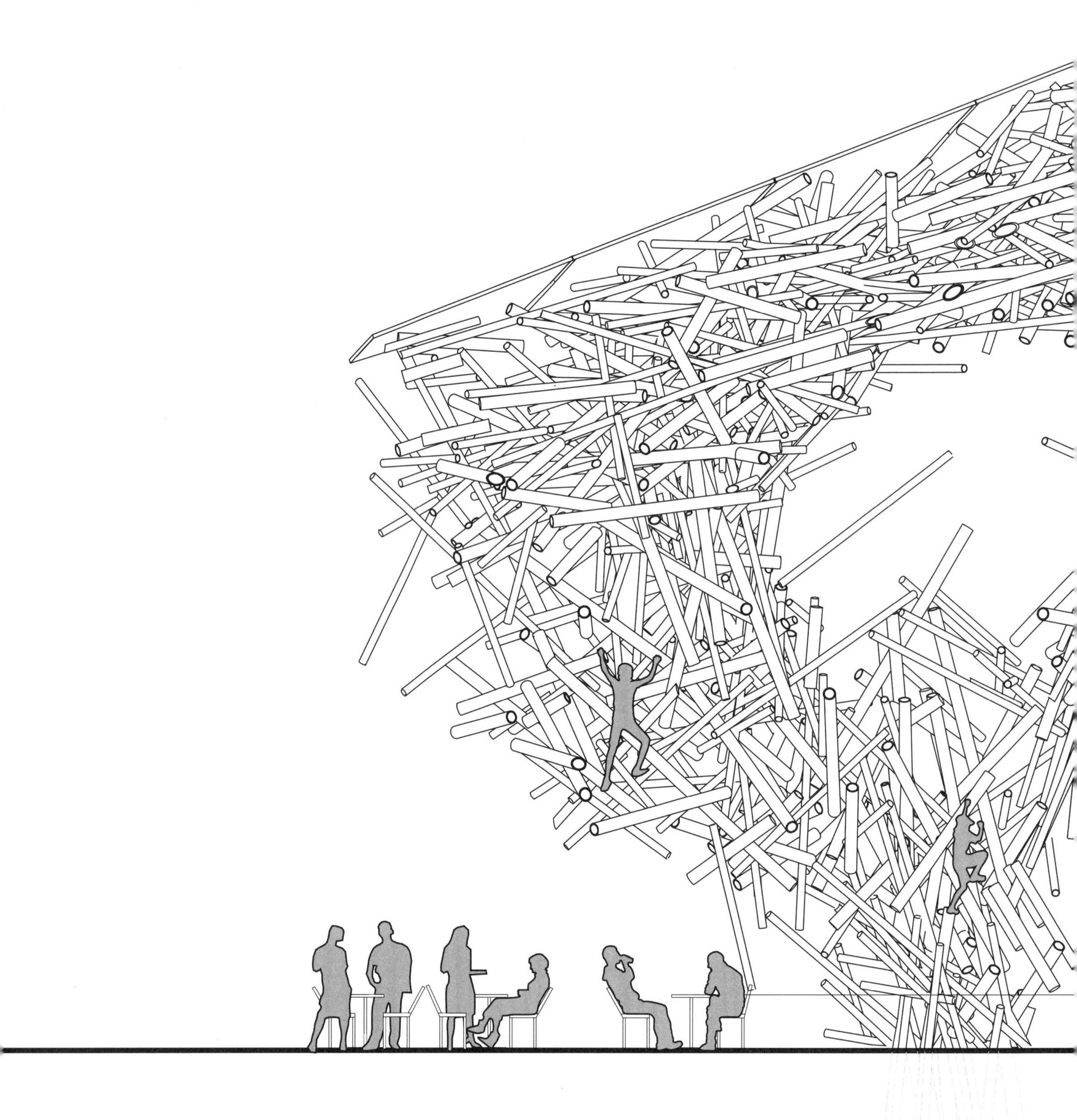

section

0 1 2 3 4 5 10m

spatial configuration studies scale 1:50

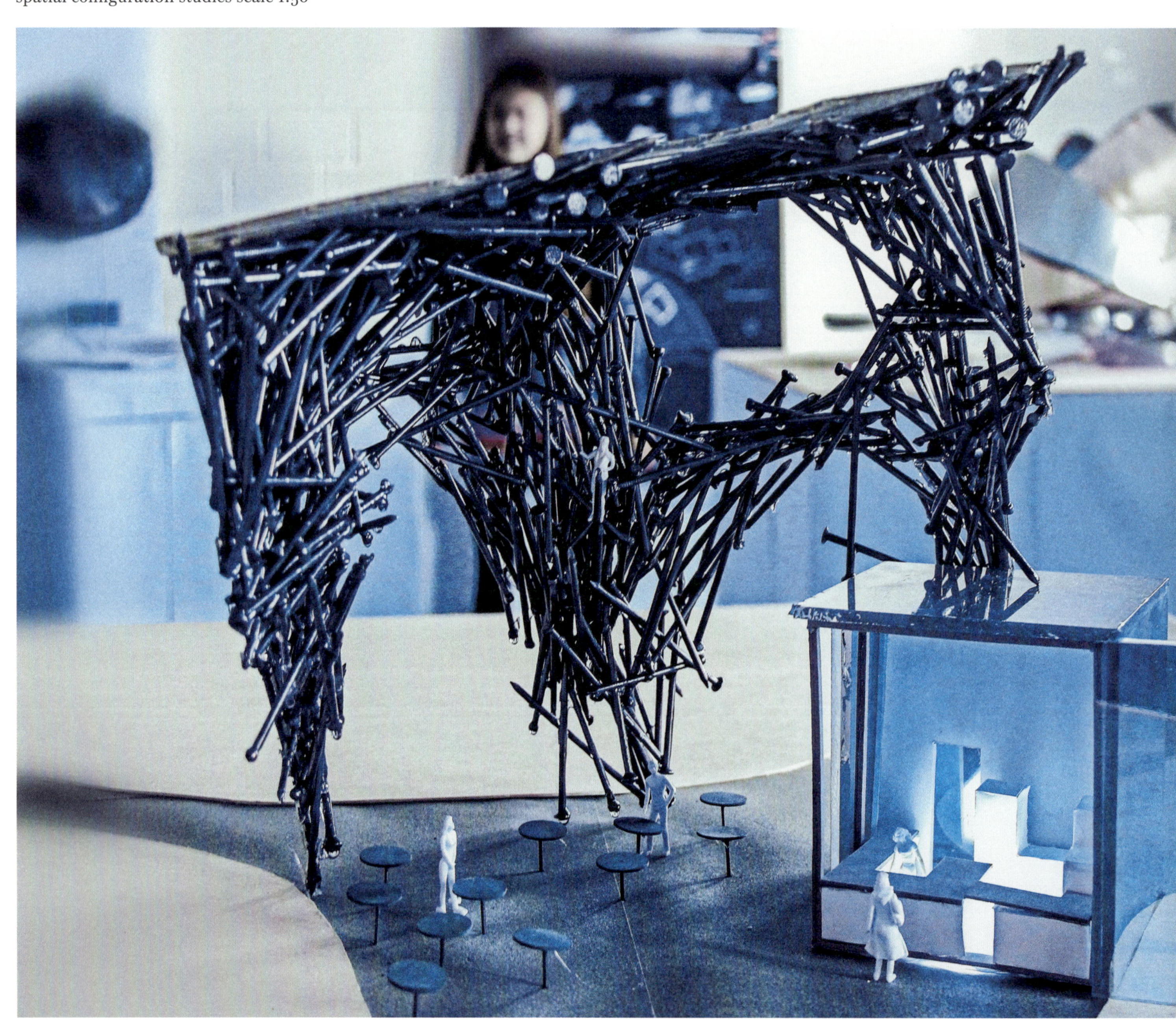

magnetic structure studies

1

2

3
8

7

1 Fondation Prada, OMA
2 Fondazione Querini Stampalia, Carlo Scarpa
3 Palazzo Grassi, Tadao Ando
4 Nordic Pavillon, BuroHappold & AaltoUniversity
5 Arsenale, Transsolar Installation
6 Palazzo Grassi, Doug Wheeler Installation
7 EEK First Year Students @ Piazza San Marco
8 Frank Stepper @ Punta della Dogana, Tadao Ando
9 Tese-ISMAR CNR, Alberto Cochetto
10 Pavillon of Italy, Elements, Rem Koolhaas

Experiment in Architecture, Thinking the Impossible

by Frank Stepper

Experiment in Architecture, Thinking the Impossible

By Frank Stepper

This chapter showcases projects that represent the core of a teaching philosophy developed by myself – Professor Frank Stepper – together with Asst. Professor Sarah Blahut (2019–2021), Professor Timo Carl (2012–2019), Asst. Professor Benjamin Jourdan (2005–2011), and Asst. Professor Astrid Lückel (2003–2005) at the Department of Experimental Design at the University of Kassel, Germany.

Architecture is the design and invention of the built environment. As an impure discipline, architecture has no inherent objectivity – there are no right and wrong answers. Scientific researchers (e.g. of natural laws) are seekers who rely on provable results to corroborate or refute a hypothesis. Architects, artists, and designers, on the other hand, are finders who think the impossible and do not follow this scientific approach. As Pablo Picasso said, "I don't seek, I find."[1]

Exploring methods for findings was the focus of the Department of Experimental Design where we Developed our teaching philosophy, thus raising the question as to what methods best enable the encountering of unpredictable shapes.

Impossible thinking means following paths of open-ended exploration and the absence of pre-conceived assumptions. By thinking the impossible one discards the rote application of overused rules and programs. Instead, an experimental process leads to surprising outcomes. As a result, innovative and unforeseeable design solutions emerge. This process, however, is not simple. The inherent want for certainty results in the inclination to be seekers and not finders.

To overcome this reflex for certainty, the focus of our teaching philosophy awakens and develops the aesthetic and formal imagination of our students through experimental actions.

The semester begins with one or more analogue experiments followed by the transformation of those experiments into video and photographic documentations. The following iterations explore the original experiment through architectural models and drawings superimposed with technical aspects. The studio courses are taught with both an intensive individual supervision of the students and teamwork training. Classes are configured to group BA and MA students within one vertical studio.

Today, in the face of growing food, migration, and climate crises, there is more need than ever for architects, artists, and designers to look beyond known solutions and push accepted boundaries. Our students, trained in impossible thinking, are uniquely positioned as finders to interact with the world as an experimental laboratory in order to discover unforeseeable design solutions for these and other critical issues.

Frank Stepper,
Vienna, Austria
July, 2023

1 Graham Sutherland quoting Picasso in 1936 in an article titled "A Trend in English Draughtsmanship" https://www.tate.org.uk/tate-etc/issue-24-spring-2012/i-do-not-seek-picasso-i-find

Vertical City

Vertical structures, such as Le Corbusier's vision of the Ville Radieuse or the skyscrapers of the American city, are landmarks of modernity. Rem Koolhaas describes in *Delirious New York* the potential of these building typologies as a way to multiply the surface of the earth and to create new worlds (e.g. Tyrell Corporation in Blade Runner, or the Tower of Babel in Metropolis).

Vertical structures are both iconic objects and, due to their size, urban building blocks. By stacking floor plans, either individually or overlapping, multifunctional and hybrid typologies are created. In particular, the overlapping of different uses facilitates the development of novel spatial and architectural qualities. Successful examples are the vehicle test track on the roof of the Fiat factory in Turin, or John Portman's public vertical atriums in the USA in the 1960s and 1970s, which were created in response to the crisis in American inner cities.

The vertical city studio takes up the hybrid and multifunctional theme for a specific location in the city of Vienna and for the sub-function "vertical farming". The city of Vienna is growing, land prices are rising, and there is an increasing need for public spaces and urban food production. The concept is that vertical farming and edible green spaces can be combined with other functions that include public spaces for recreation and communication within a multifunctional vertical city.

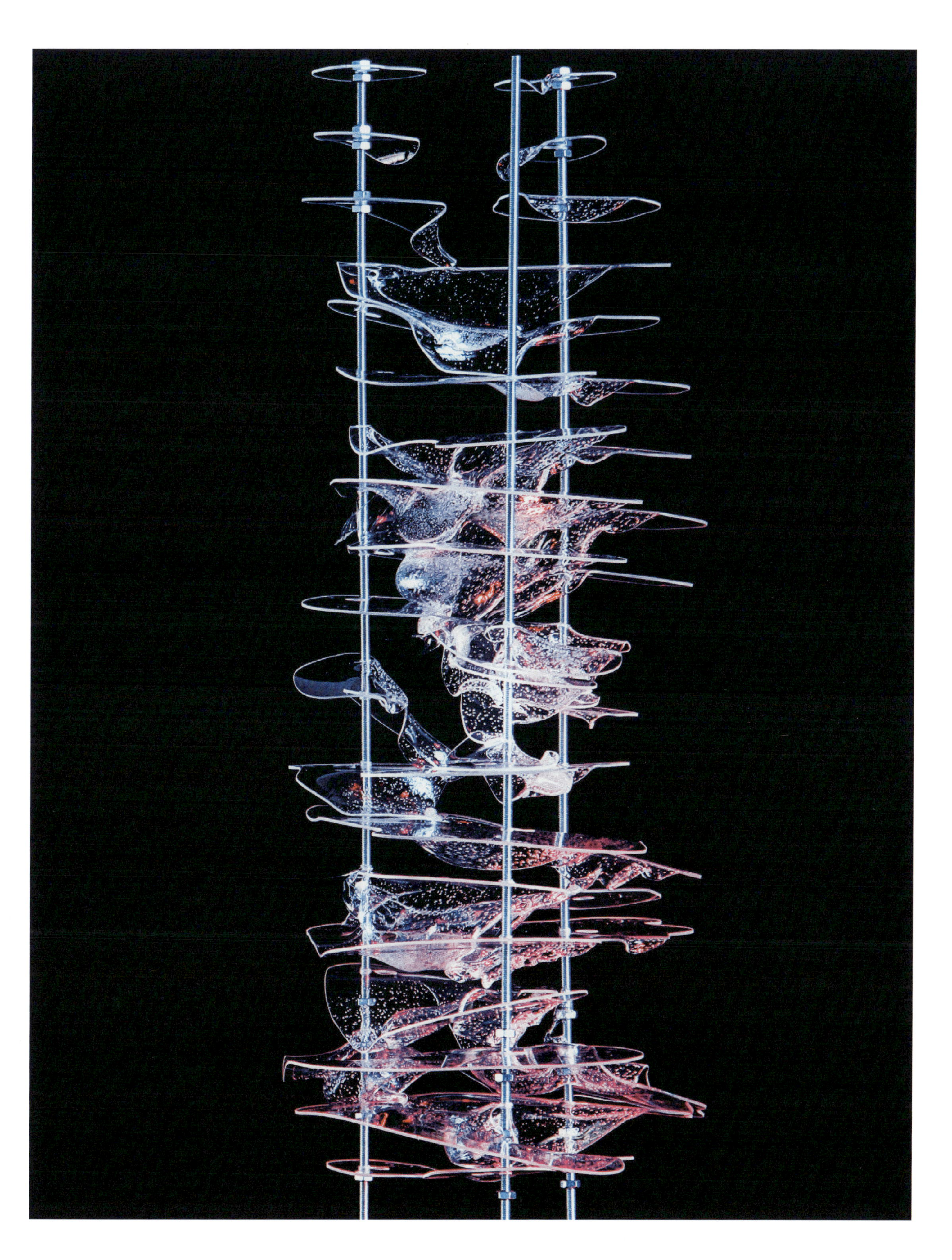

EXPERIMENT
↙ VIDEO

Project: Jupiter Clouds, 2018
by Julian Fiegehenn, Philipp Pusceddu
Experiment "Thermoplastic Metamorphosis"

sky bridges and vertical public plazas

Project: Vertical Wave, 2018
by Ran Li, Yunjie Chung
Experiment "gravity flow with paper"

start

end

folded space

Project: Vertical Wave, 2018

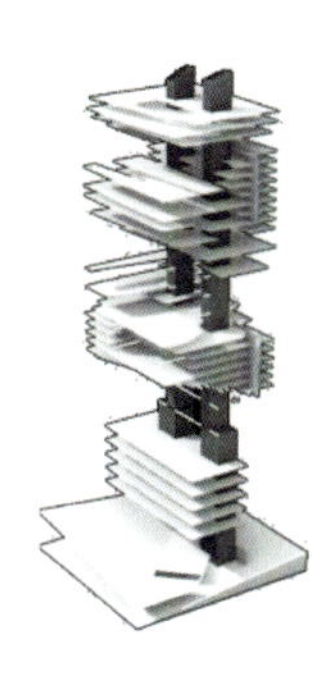

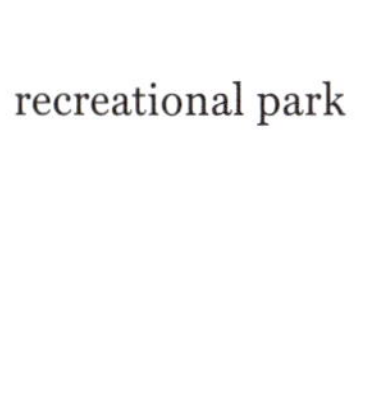

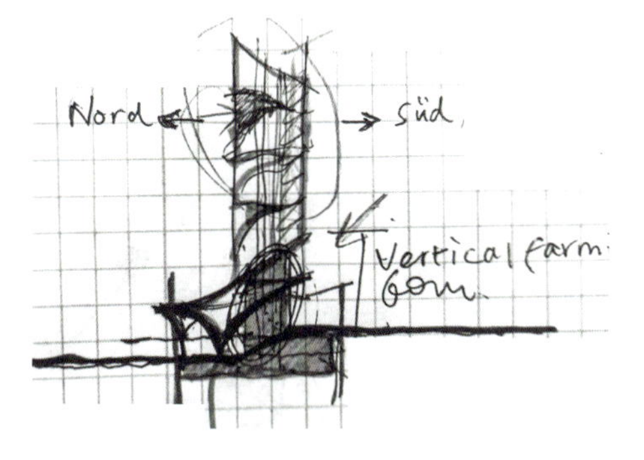

recreational park

edible park

family farm

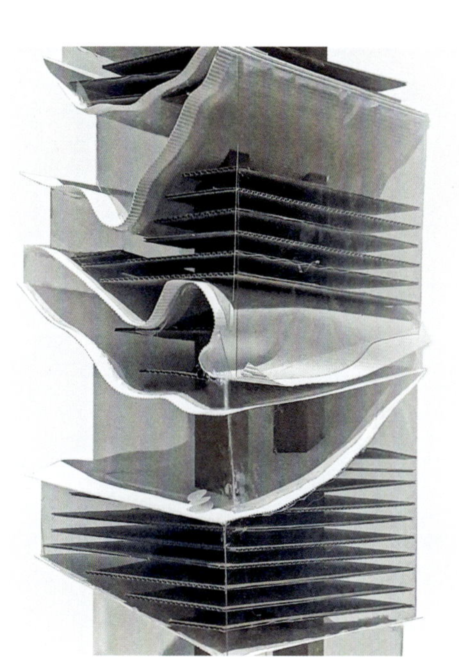

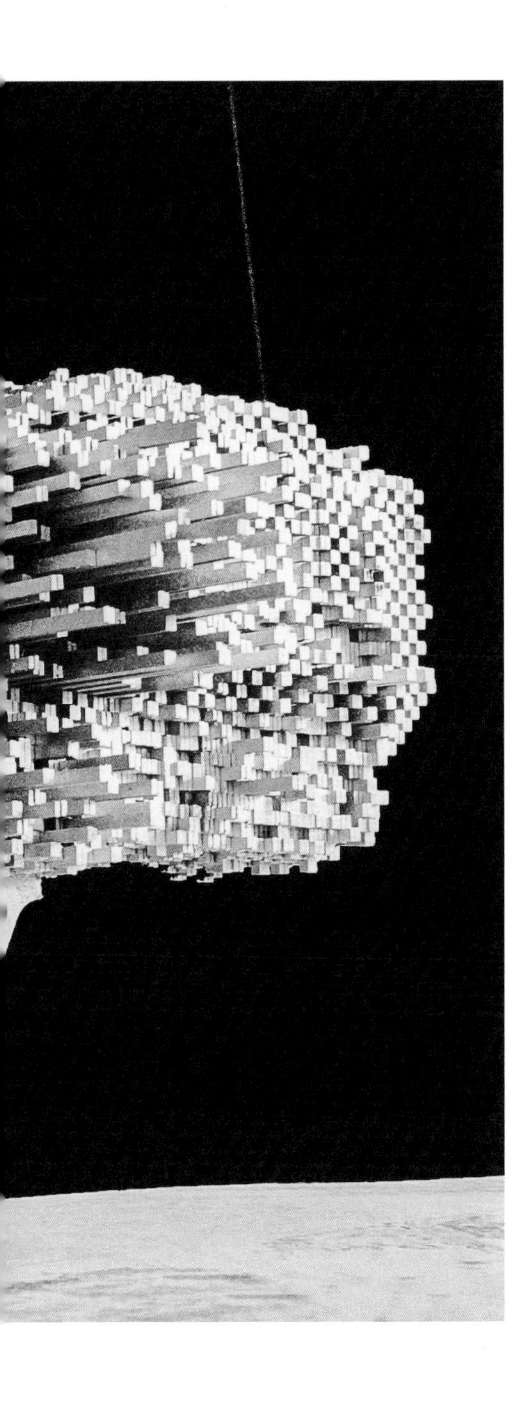

Berlin Tegel Airport

Set in the context of the former Berlin Tegel airport, Flyscraper is a modular post-fossil fuel city structure that can grow and shrink flexibly. It is a pixelated organism that provides a habitat for around 1.2 million people. A module, one pixel, has the dimensions of 25 × 25 × 25 m and can contain up to five floors, each with 625 sqm. The individual living modules are basically designed as a shared flat, as multi-generational units, and are grouped around semi-public and public squares.

The city sculpture is traversed in the middle by a functional organ, an open space that accommodates both cultural and leisure activities. It also serves as an orientation axis and connects all districts with each other. A sky window frames the view of urban Berlin in the east and opens up a view of Brandenburg's nature in the west. A large opening in the top third of the sculpture forms a central park. In addition, the structure is criss-crossed with vertical atriums.

Public transport consists of a system of tubes in which gyroscopic capsules move that are held in place by a magnetic field. The exposed outer surfaces of the energy modules are equipped with photovoltaic panels and wind power is generated in the center of each energy module via a wind turbine. To ensure energy autonomy two wind tunnels run through the center of Flyscraper from west to east. The central waste collection and recycling system is located between these wind tunnels. Similar to the energetic structure of Flyscraper, the old airfield is divided into a grid of 25 × 25 m and is also used for energy and food production.

Thus, Flyscraper functions as a self-contained, self-sufficient urban system that, with its efficient resource management, is capable of providing not only for itself but for all of Berlin.

Project: Flyscraper, 2012
by Ernesto M. Mulch, Stefan Niggemeyer

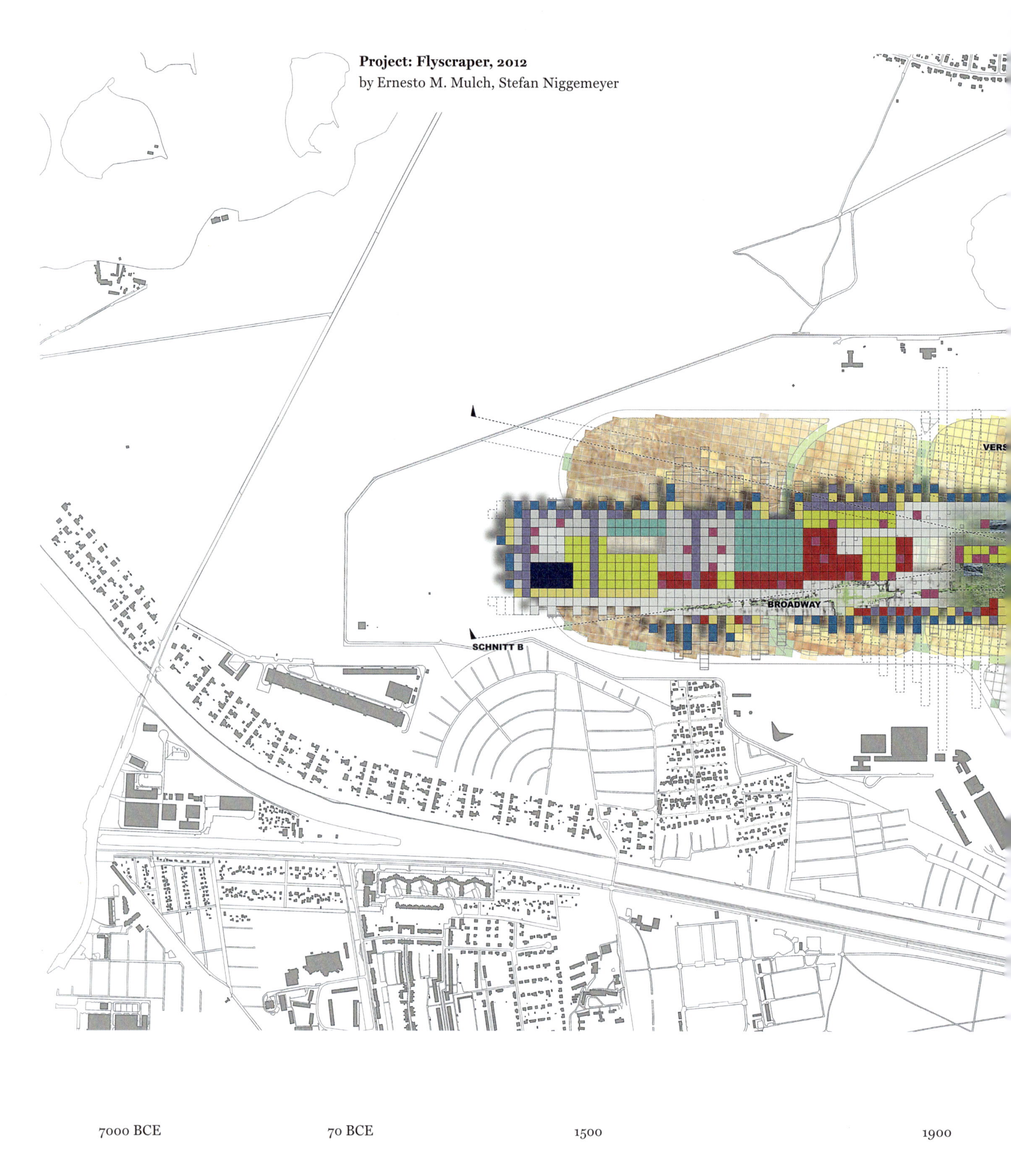

7000 BCE

70 BCE

1500

1900

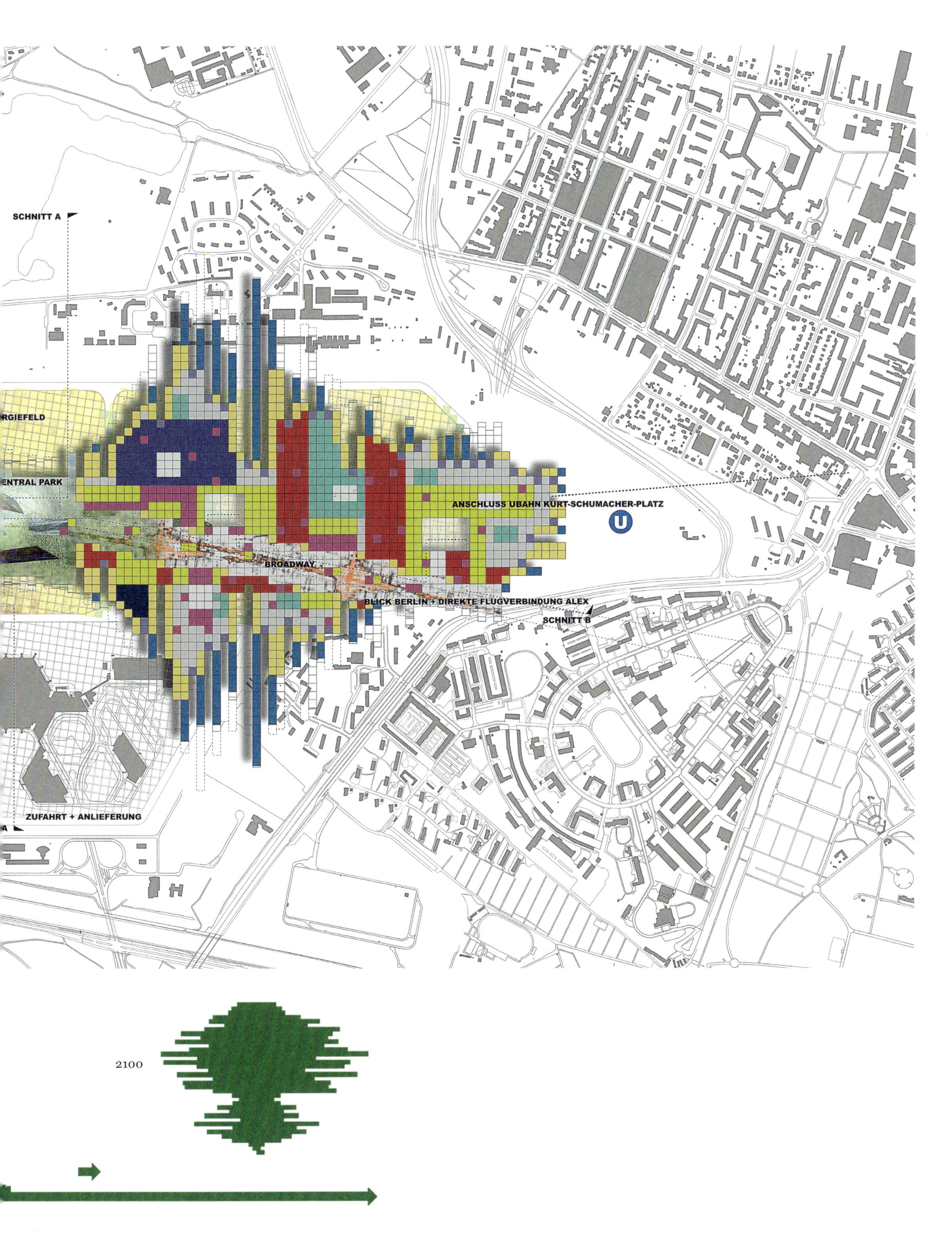
SCHNITT A
RGIEFELD
ENTRAL PARK
ANSCHLUSS UBAHN KURT-SCHUMACHER-PLATZ
U
BROADWAY
BLICK BERLIN + DIREKTE FLUGVERBINDUNG ALEX
SCHNITT B
ZUFAHRT + ANLIEFERUNG
A
2100

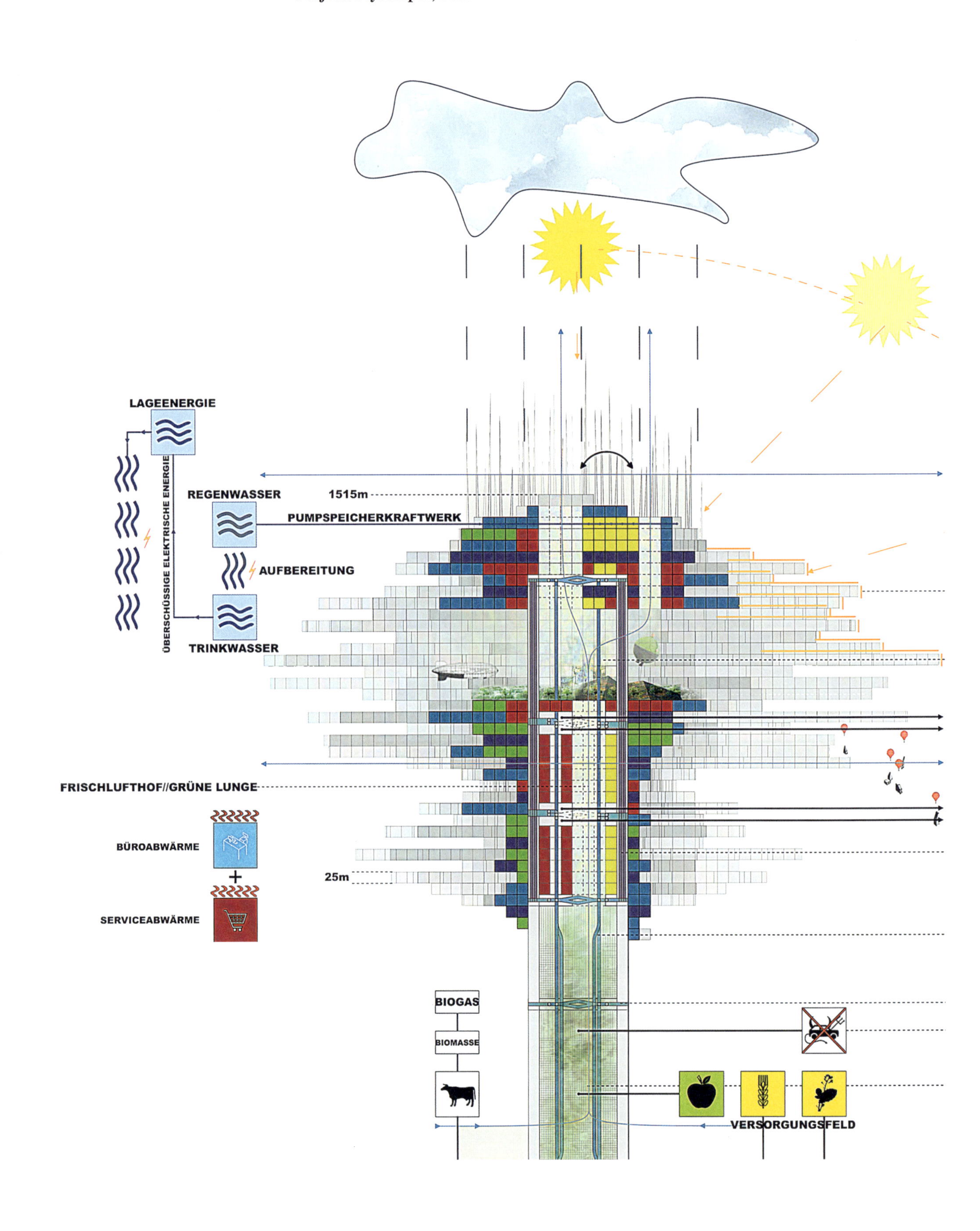
LAGEENERGIE
ÜBERSCHÜSSIGE ELEKTRISCHE ENERGIE
REGENWASSER
1515m
PUMPSPEICHERKRAFTWERK
AUFBEREITUNG
TRINKWASSER
FRISCHLUFTHOF//GRÜNE LUNGE
BÜROABWÄRME
+
SERVICEABWÄRME
25m
BIOGAS
BIOMASSE
VERSORGUNGSFELD

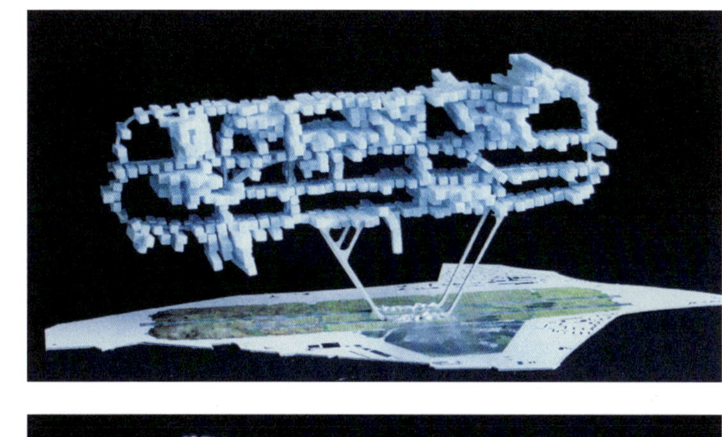

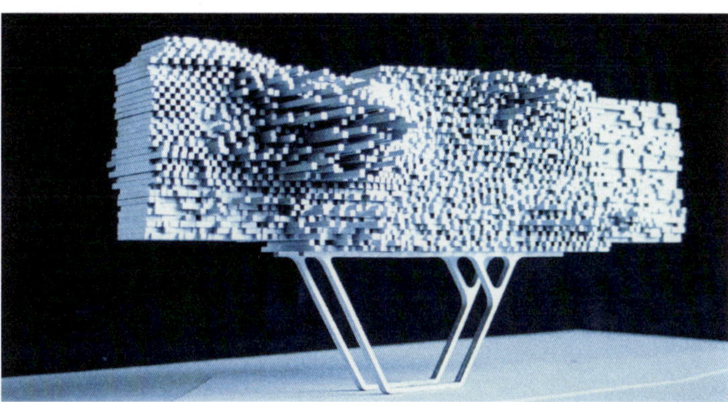

growth pattern

Project: Flyscraper, 2012

collage energy landscape

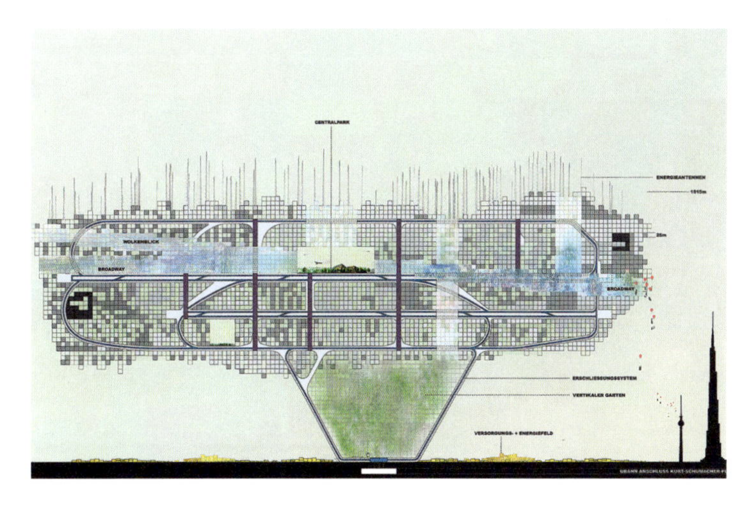

circulation and green space diagram

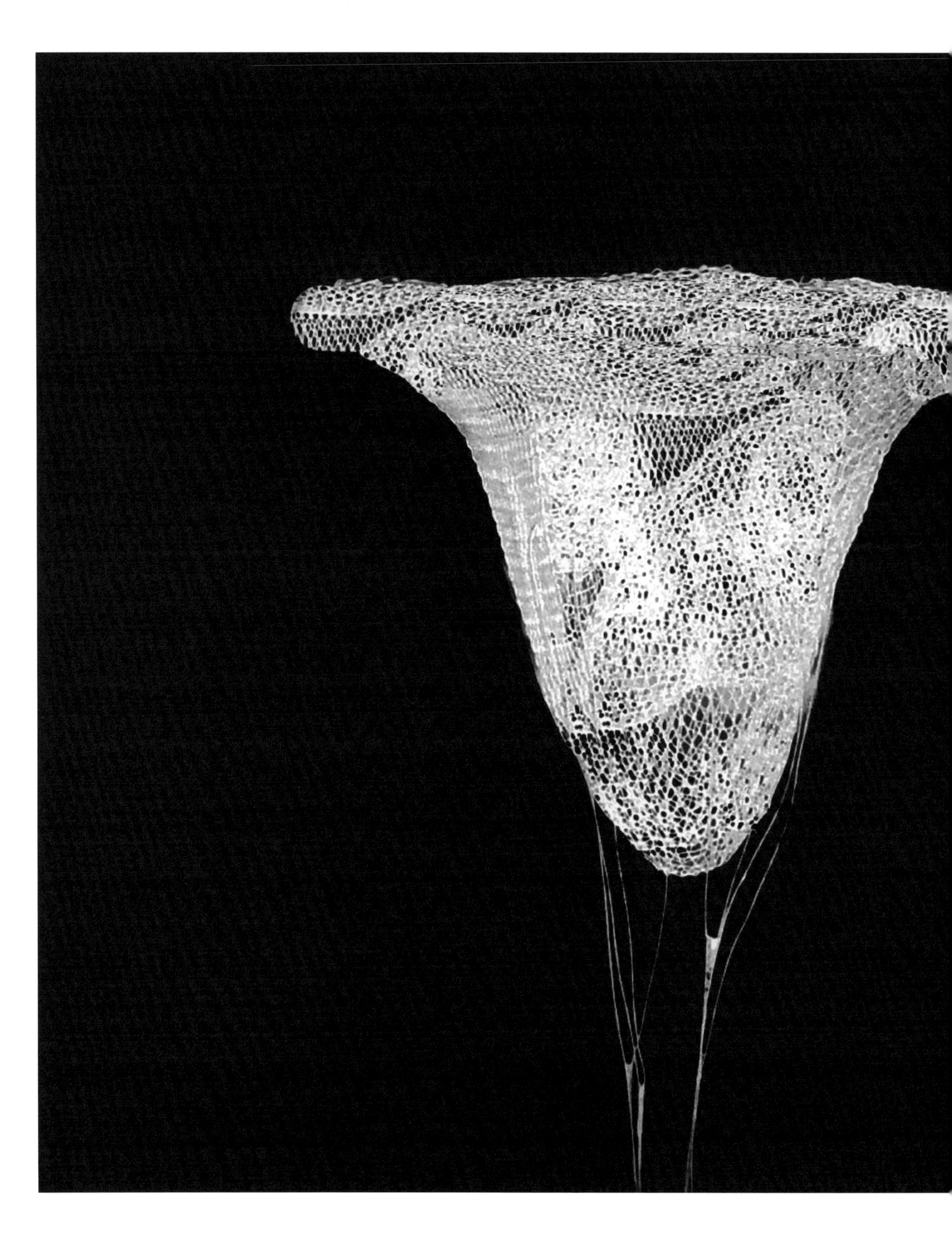

Land Unter

The studio Land Under engages with the sinking of a distant atoll in the Pacific, located in the middle of the ocean between Australia and the US. There, corals have formed circular archipelagos over thousands of years: Majuro in the Marshall Islands.

While the 2015 climate summit in Paris was still negotiating how much climate temperature change is acceptable, the rising sea level in this paradise of azure blue water and palm trees is already causing fields to dry out and the groundwater to become salty. Centimeter by centimeter, the residents are being deprived of their livelihood. A nation without a country is not yet recognized as a "climate refugee".

Rising sea levels are threatening the homes of more than 150 million people in coastal regions worldwide.

This all too real dystopia sets the framework for designing novel sustainable and spatial urban planning scenarios. The status quo of what is feasible today (floating houses and cities, artificial islands, dams, etc.) plays is combined with the development of one's own spatial utopia in the tradition of Archigram and Lebbeus Woods. Students developed ideas for resilient and self-supporting floating or bridge-like infrastructures that grow over time, considering economic, ecological, social, urban, and architectural parameters.

Project: Elastic Architecture, 2016
by Zhikai Feng
Experiment “Elastic Space”

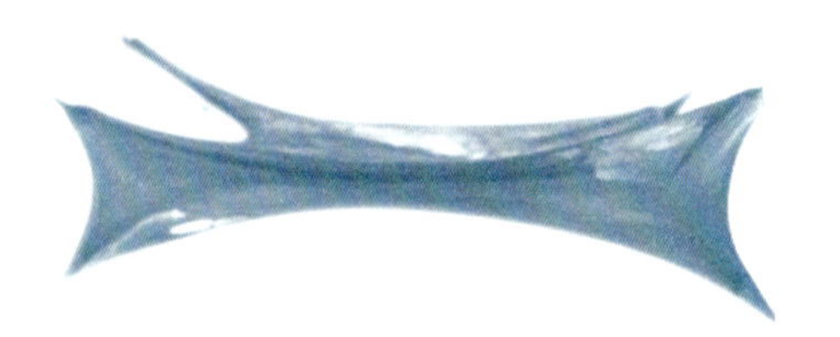

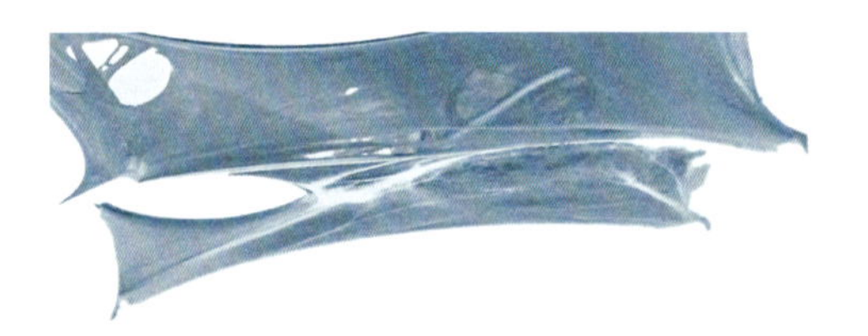

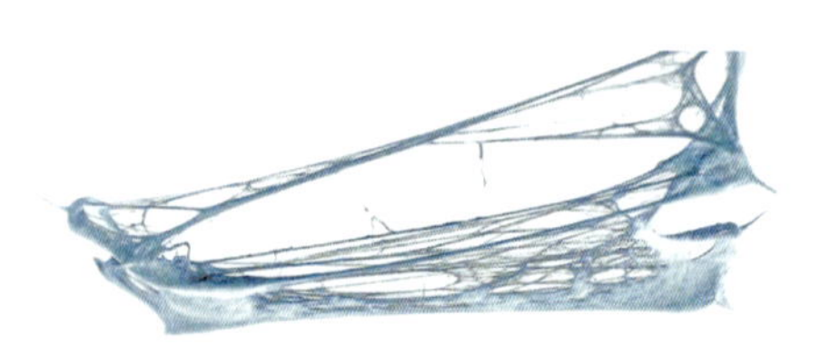

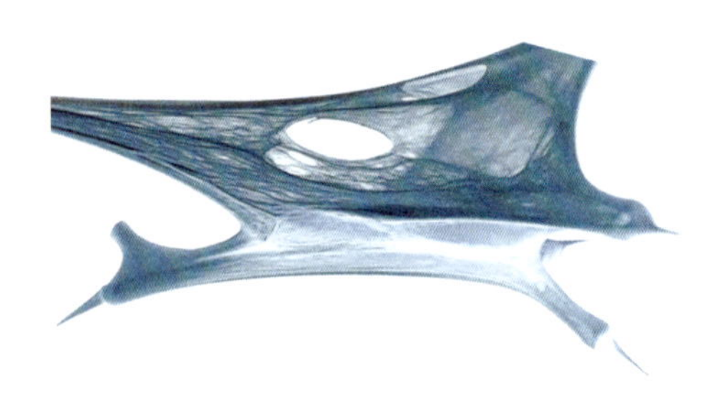

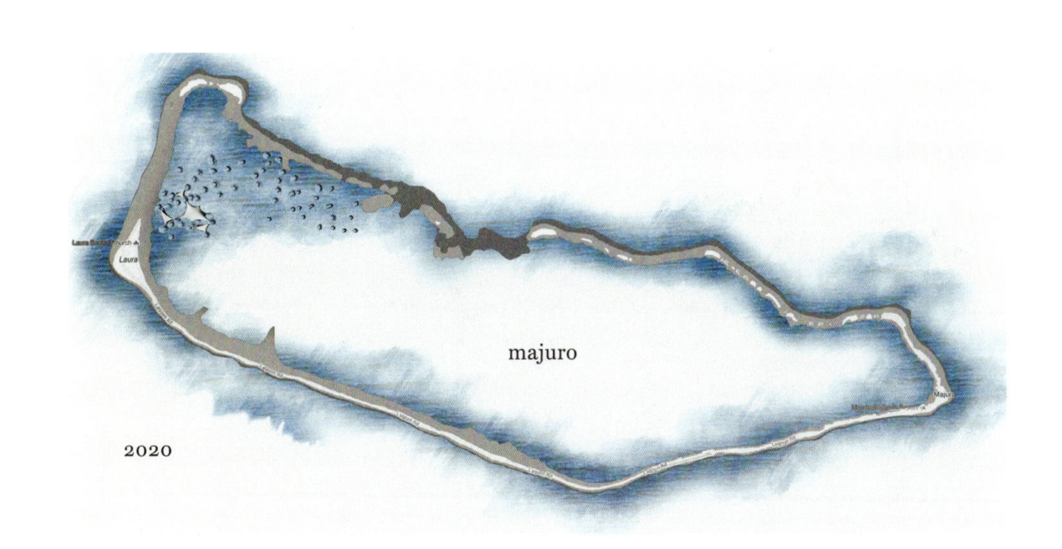
majuro
2020

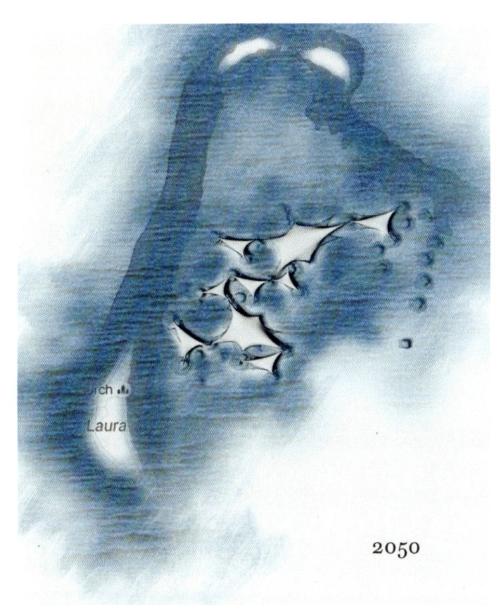
Laura
2050

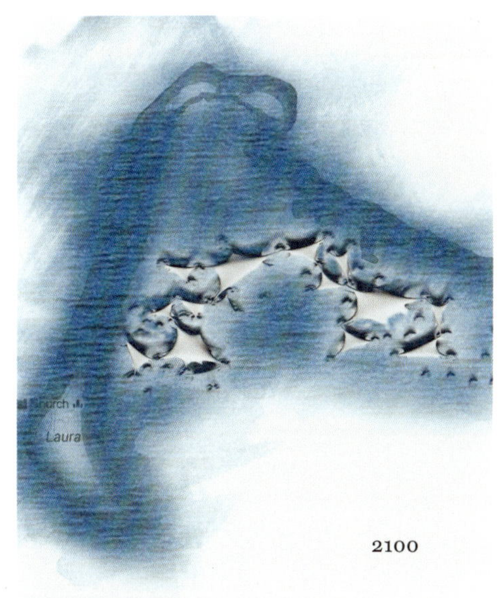
Laura
2100

Project: Deep Growth, 2016
by Elena Matveev
Experiment "Liquid Space"

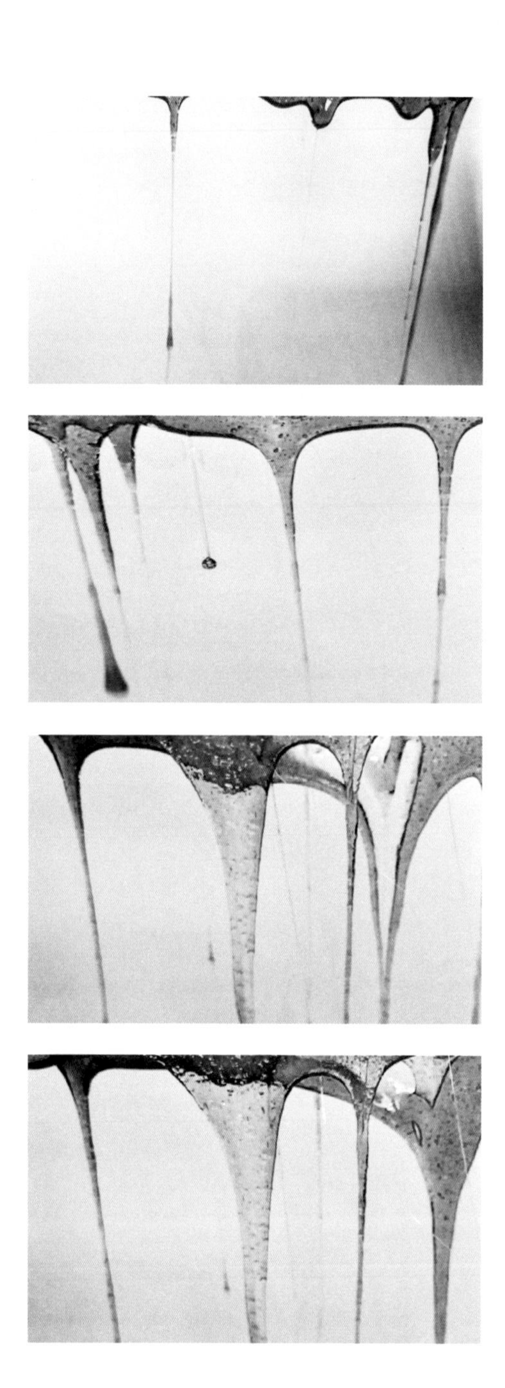

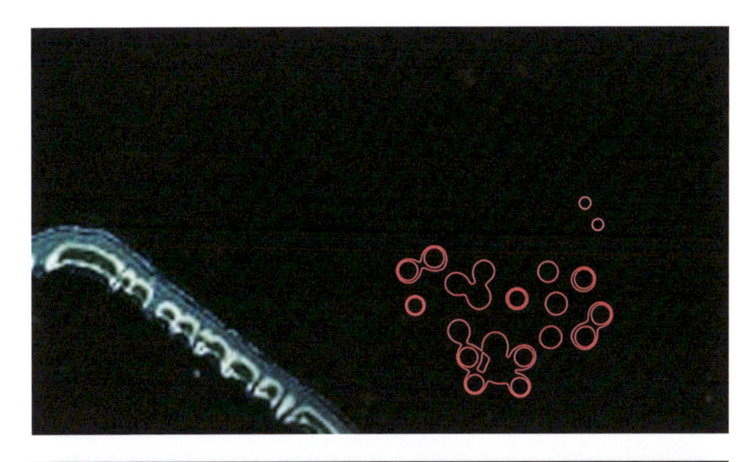

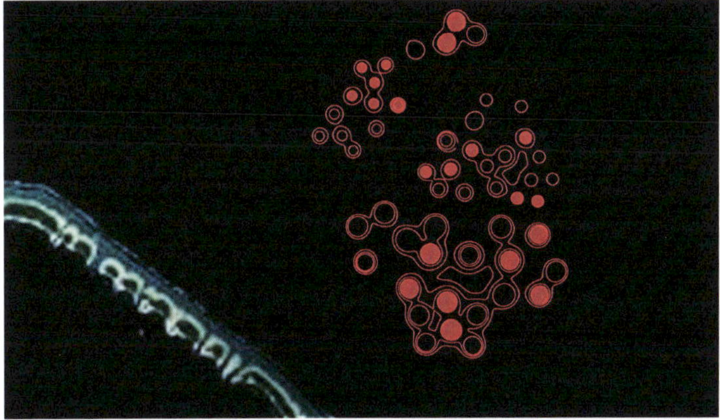

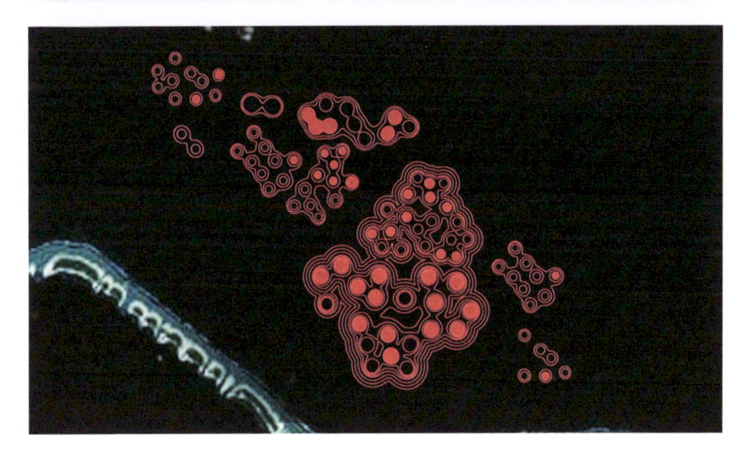

growth process

The core of this concept lies in a series of measures to develop the islands into a unit that is economically, ecologically, and energy self-sufficient.

The problem of water supply is solved with a rain water collection, treatment, storage, and purification system. The required infrastructure is installed inside the chambers provided within the island unit.

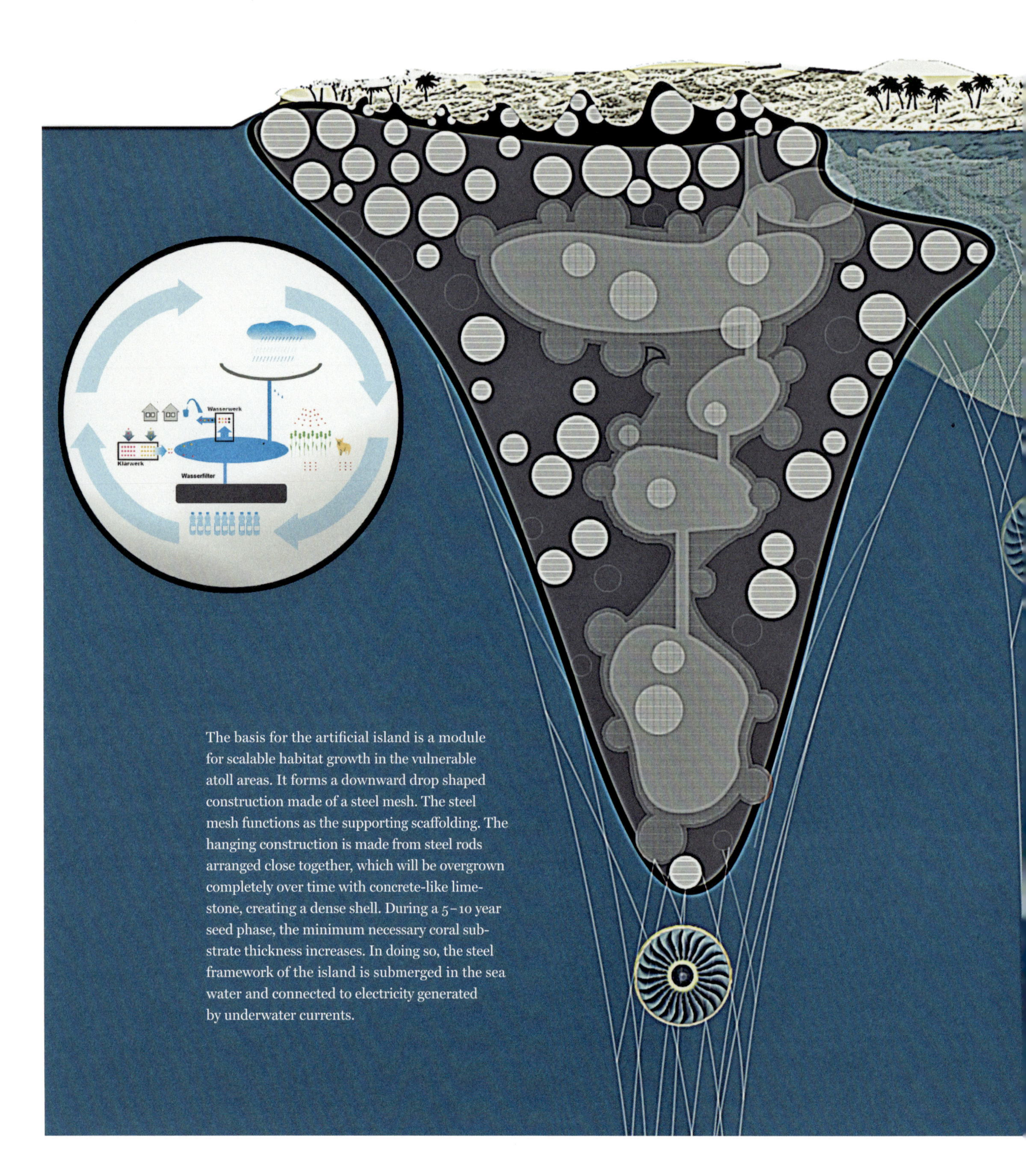

The basis for the artificial island is a module for scalable habitat growth in the vulnerable atoll areas. It forms a downward drop shaped construction made of a steel mesh. The steel mesh functions as the supporting scaffolding. The hanging construction is made from steel rods arranged close together, which will be overgrown completely over time with concrete-like limestone, creating a dense shell. During a 5–10 year seed phase, the minimum necessary coral substrate thickness increases. In doing so, the steel framework of the island is submerged in the sea water and connected to electricity generated by underwater currents.

The tourism industry forms the central development direction for securing economic independence. Underwater landscapes with coral colonies and the associated biological diversity offer development potential for tourist activities.

Guggenheim Helsinki

The point of departure for this studio is the competition for a new museum building in Helsinki's South Harbor organized by the Guggenheim Foundation. The city of Helsinki is speculating on a "Bilbao effect" to create a new nexus for tourism and art through the construction of an iconic museum building. Such a museum typology moves in the field of tension between extravagance and local context and includes a number of varying requirements: Art container, art education, functional sculpture, cultural institution, as well as the creation of urban semi-public spaces. The wide range of contemporary museum buildings is a testament to this predicament. Contemporary museum typologies range from bourgeois educational institutions to commercialized theme parks. Today, museums can be a reservoir for thoughts, places of auratic objects, as well as flexible and public institutions in the urban realm.

We asked students to take a stance and reflect on the institution of the museum: fast food art or à la carte art? / public or private? / minimalist or expressionist? Maybe even something wonderful in between.

Project: Synthesystem, 2014
by Andreas Göbert, Patrick Euler
Experiment "Magnetic Ink"

investigation between hard
and soft space

Project: Synthesystem, 2014

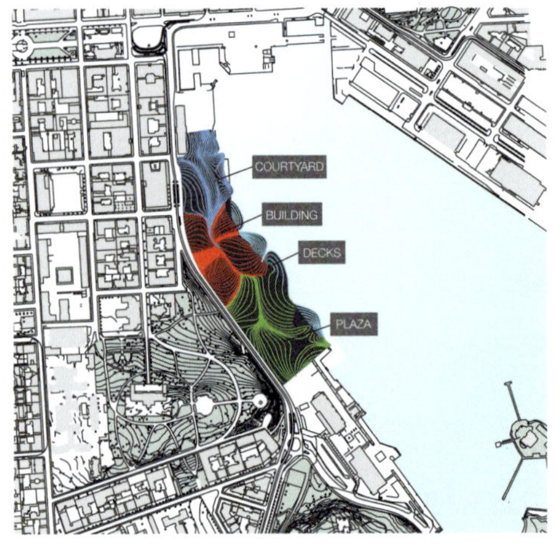

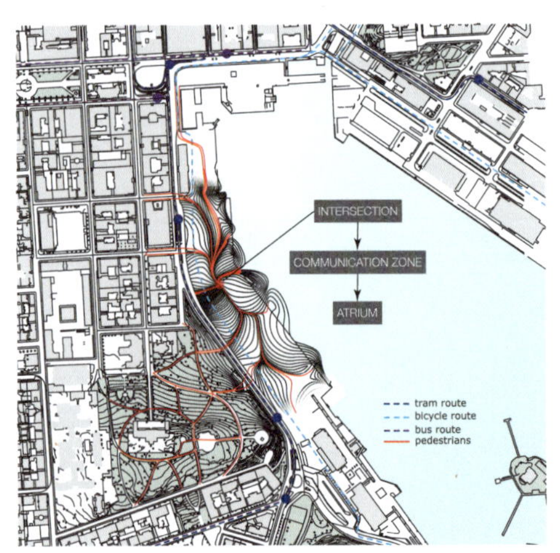

site attractors

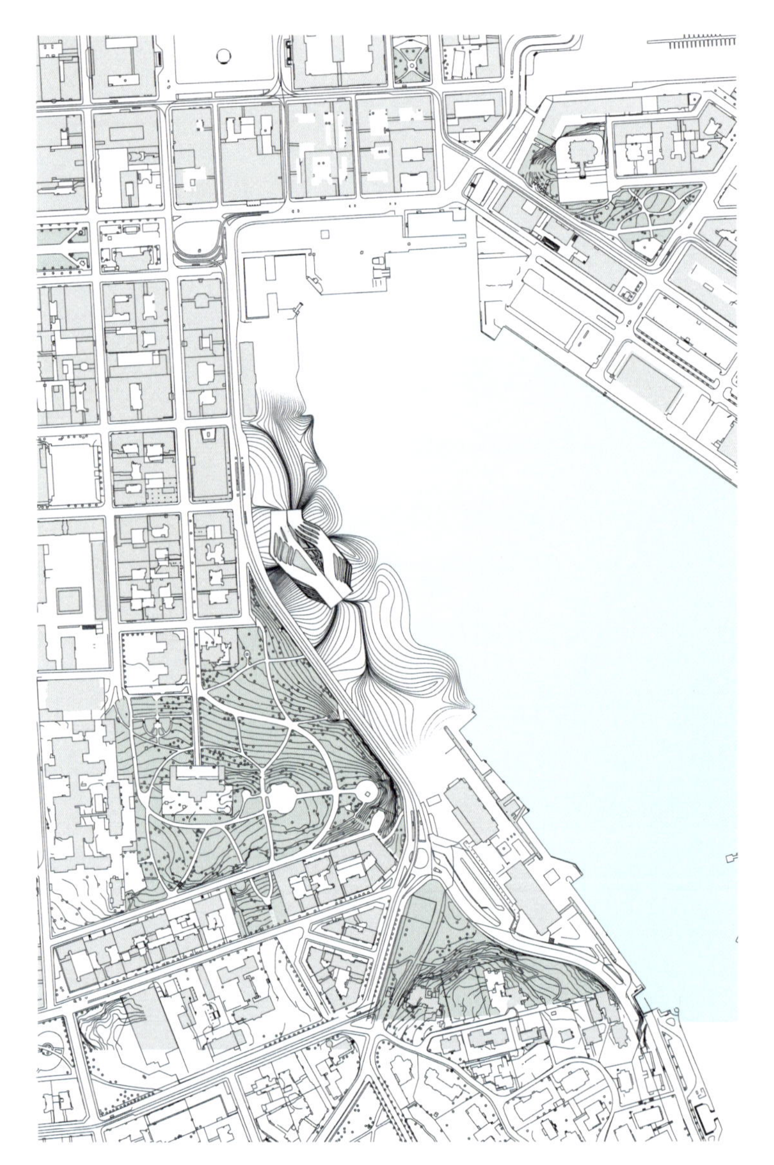

site plan

The initial ideas on the complex space program for the museum establish an arrangement of the rooms as individual, yet connected, satellites. The arrangement of the program was positioned in the form of a deformed donut with an interior atrium designed to have criss-crossing ramps that are used as shortcuts. The compact arrangement model splits into two strands with an articulation of a soft inner core. The exhibition areas are mostly oriented around the huge atrium to intensify the interior communication and vistas, whereas restaurant and cafe, event and multifunctional areas, and open office spaces are oriented to the sea-side and plazas for sufficient daylight and an inside-out relationship.

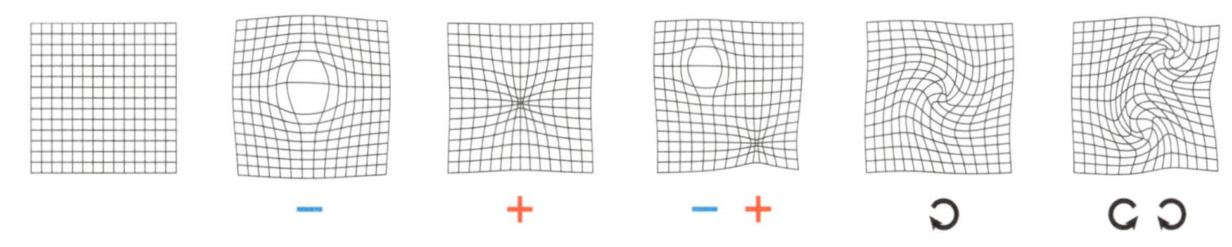

2D visualization of attraction and repulsion

3D formfinding model of attraction and repulsion

Project: Synthesystem, 2014

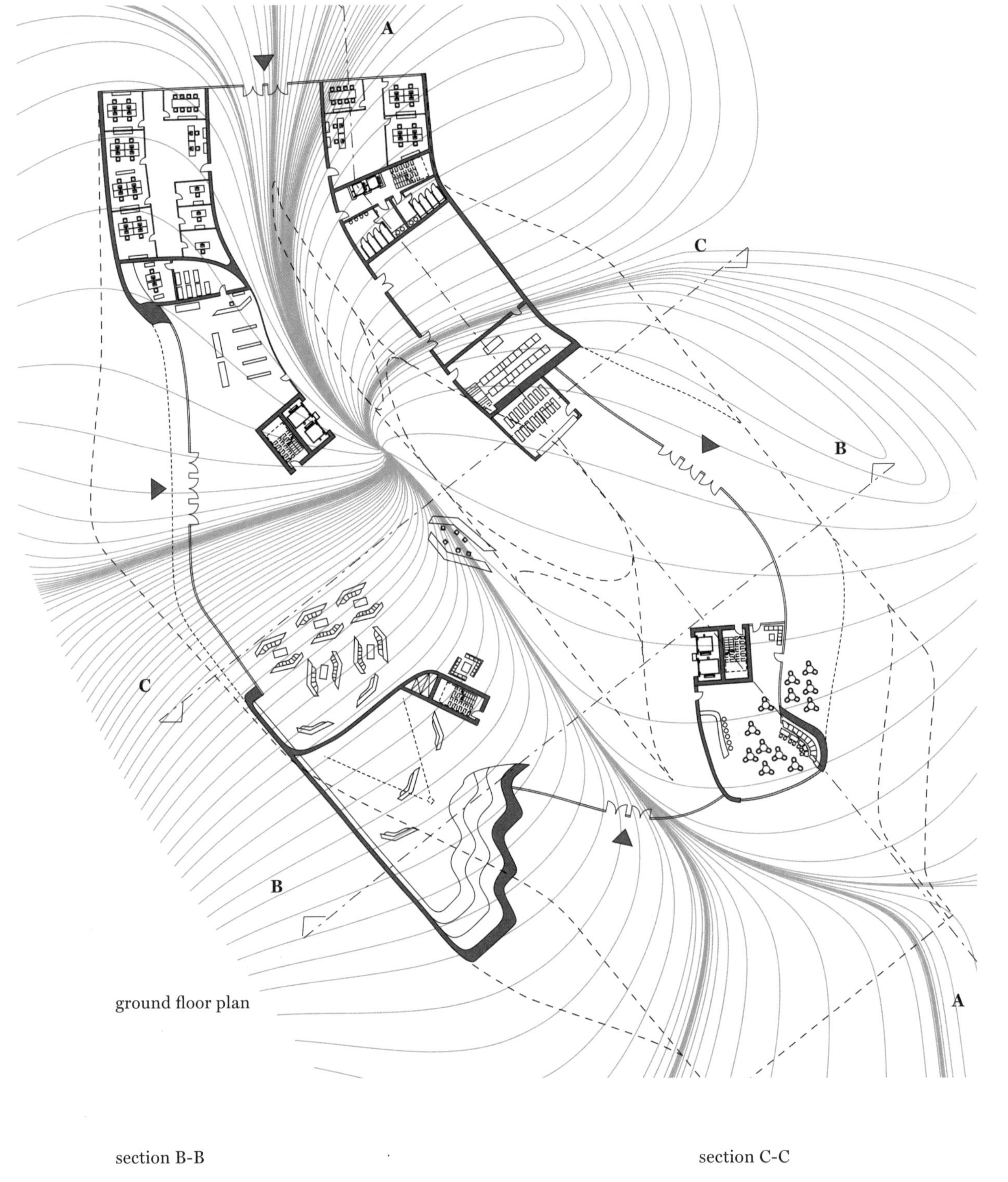

ground floor plan

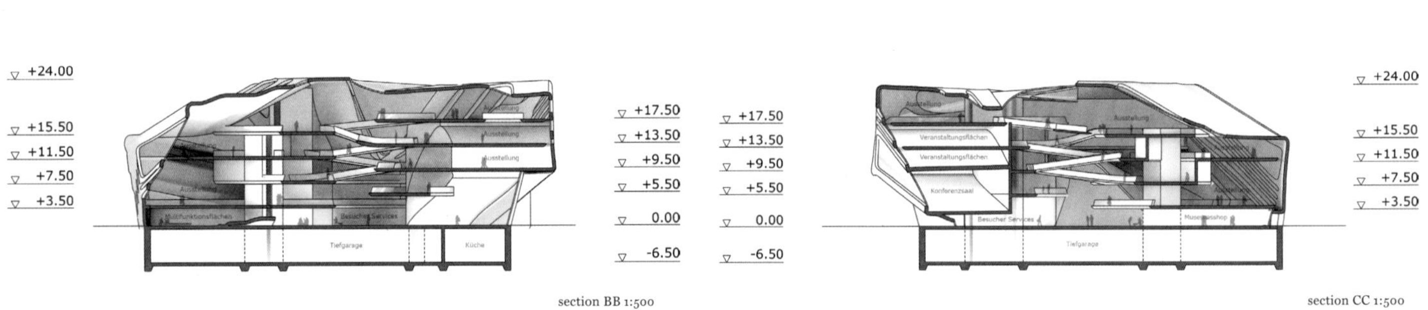

section BB 1:500

section CC 1:500

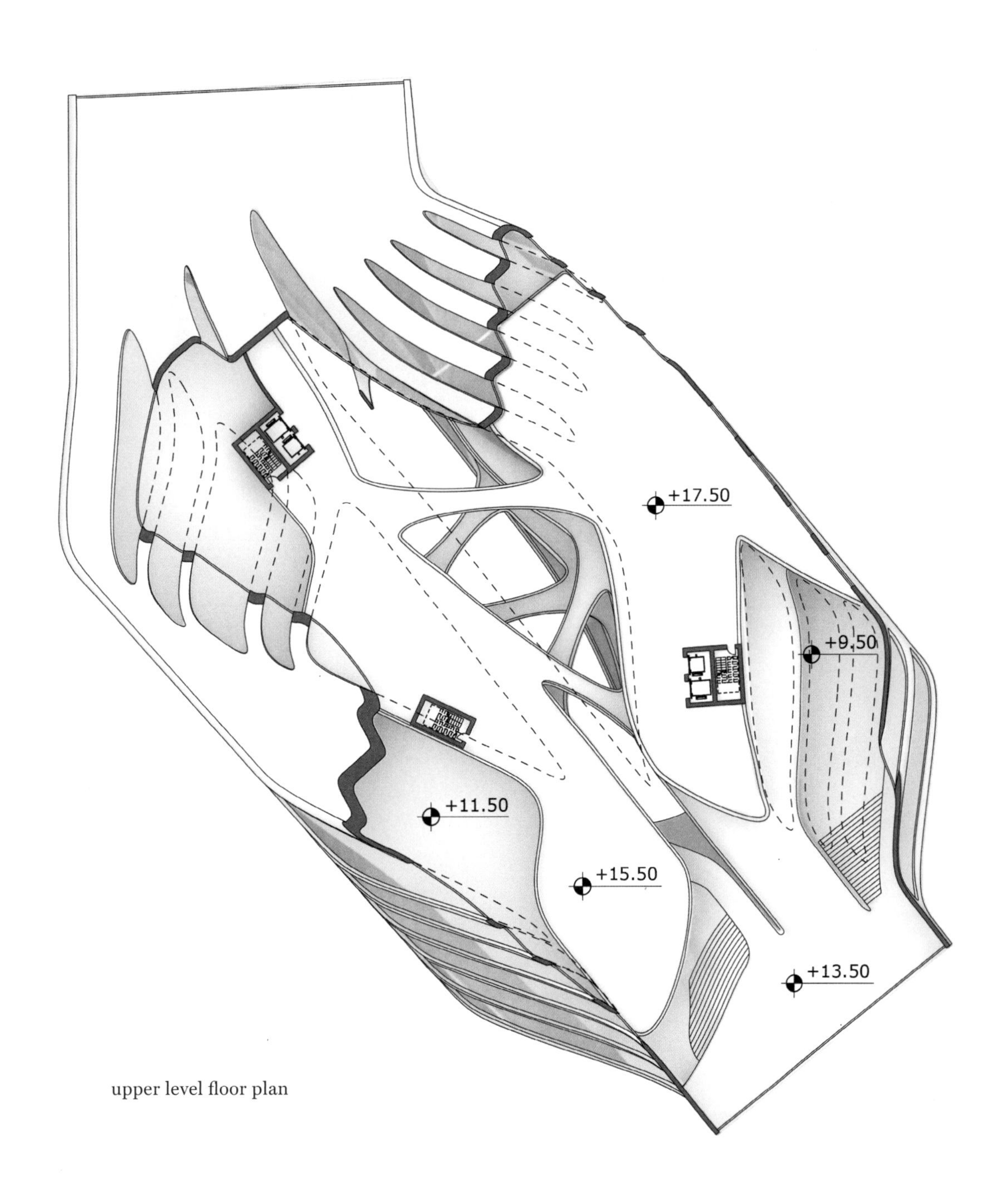

upper level floor plan

section A-A

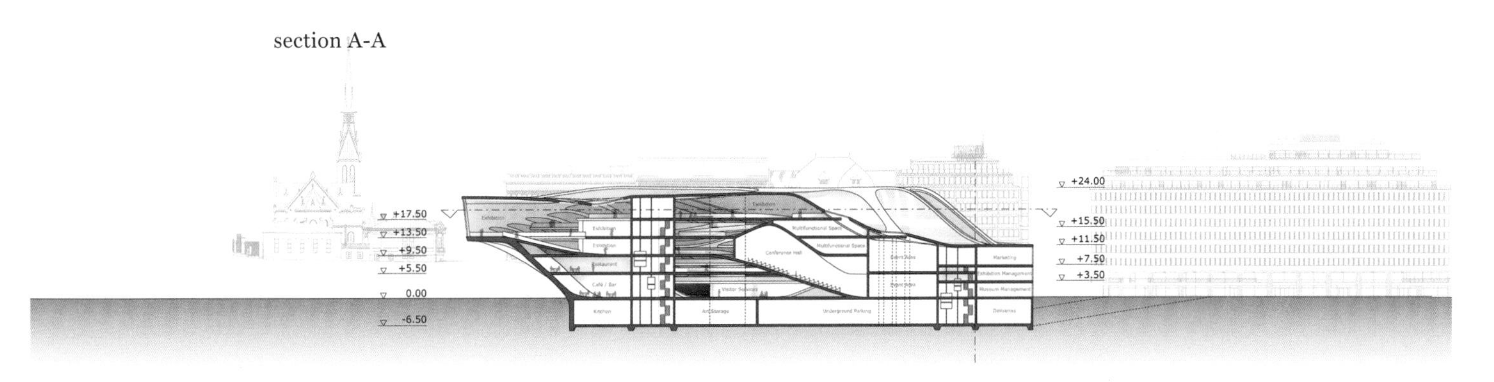

Project: Synthesystem, 2014

main atrium

exhibition space

exhibition space

Project: Synthesystem, 2014

section model with context

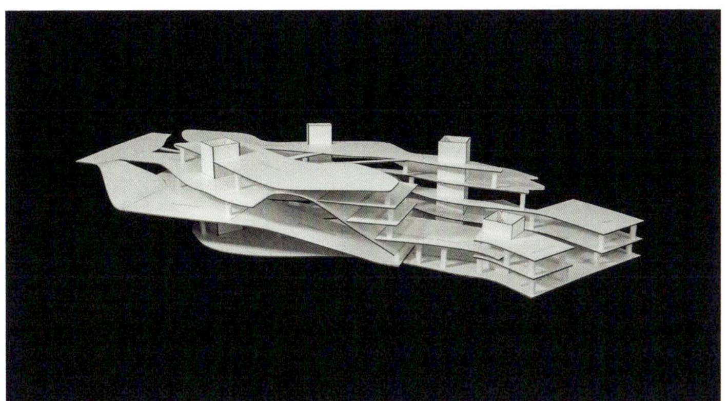

circulation model

section model with context

1
2
3
7
8
9

4

5

6

10

11

Experimenting with Real World Parameters

by Timo Carl

Experimenting with Real World Parameters

By Timo Carl

This chapter focuses on experimentation within research through design & making[1] studios and seminars.

Architectural research requires methods that combine both scientific rigor and design creativity. The discipline of architecture is challenging in that it links aesthetics with functional requirements, thus creating open and complex spatial solutions spaces. The results are "wicked problems" (Rittel 1976) that are impossible to quantify or to solve with a single right or wrong answer. There are just too many variables that depend on each other. The following discussion outlines a plan of attack for tackling this complexity, developed during my PhD tenure with Frank Stepper.

Considering experimentation as the predominant form of research, there are several similarities, but also distinctive features, between the role of experimentation in architecture and the sciences. Both disciplines bring about something through experimentation that does not yet exist (Marguin et al. 2019). Moreover, "Experimentation serves as an empirical structure that allows researchers to remain capable of acting in a state of not-knowing" (Rheinberger 2014). Likewise, process-driven design methods aid designers in navigating through an overwhelming space of architectural possibilities. This requires the development of routines and the definition of parameters that can be hypothesized, controlled, and measured, such as the physical scale models of Frei Otto (Kotnik 2011). At the same time, architectural experiments need to involve great openness and an elemental core of creativity. While repeatability is elemental in scientific experiments (e.g., in physics), in architecture the singular object resulting from the design process is of particular interest for gaining knowledge.

Frank eloquently coined the German term *Funktionsplastik* (English: functional sculpture) to reconcile the apparent contradiction between hypothesis-driven and explorative, creative methods. A notion that is flexible enough to operate beyond a single logic – material, structural, geometric, ecological, or spatial considerations.

This gives rise to an architecture that is more than the sum of its parts, namely a holistic approach to Gestalt and mode of action. The concept is a sublime variation of functionalism and follows the tradition of organic architecture (Pehnt 2004). Moreover, it provides a productive framework for the use of computational design methods and highlight Frank's interest in novel technologies which push the boundaries of architecture.

Operating within real-world scale design and build projects inevitably ties creative design practice to a series of constraints, like material properties, geometry, and fabrication processes. The design process must recognize bespoke parameters as an integral part of architectural conception from the outset. A prime example are the form-finding strategies of Frei Otto that combine the physical realms of material premise and the natural flow of forces with the formation of space. Therefore, it is essential to explore innovative design solutions through extensive testing and experimentation. However, it also takes a great deal of creativity to transgress pure material and technical constraints and to identify the right design drivers. Computational methods help designers to make informed design decisions quickly by formalizing relevant geometrical, material, and environmental or structural parameters. In our case, those digital tools constitute a loose collection of explicit and parametric geometry modeling, physical simulation, radiation analysis, and some impromptu snippets of visual programming that complement the broad range of analogue methods used.

Such a modus operandi requires the formulation of a precise research question that determines both the use of digital design and manufacturing tools, as well as the definition of definite building typologies at the beginning of an investigation. However speculative, explorative, or experimental the projects in this chapter may seem, they all rigorously foreground a specific research topic.

1 Research through design and making also known as "research through art and design" (Frayling 1999), practice-led research (Cross 2001), or "research through design" (Downton 2004) among others.

The Solar Spline project revisited traditional velas (i.e. sun sails) to reinvent them with novel energy producing materials. We followed in the footsteps of Frei Otto and introduced analogue and digital form-finding strategies as both primary research method and guardrail to limit the scope of our investigations.

The forerunner seminar Free Skin explored novel construction methods for external, lightweight shading elements with improved functionalities (solar, energy, and sensor activated lighting). In the Urban Glow seminar, we tested the combination of interactive and social behaviors temporarily reactivating lost spaces in the urban fabric of Kassel. During the Covid-19 pandemic, Sarah Blahut investigated alternative modes of representation and scale for research dealing with digital and analogue mediums for drawing translations within the context of her Lost and Found seminar.

Working with Frank, I learned the importance of the double meaning of the French word *expérience* as experiment and experience, because architecture as a discipline thrives on the capacity to make decisions, based on the synthesis of knowledge and experience (Carl 2019). Design ideas unfold or crumble at the moment of their materialization. Future architects gain valuable experience by building 1:1 scale demonstrators and by experimenting with real parameters. Conceptualizing and building those real-world experiments brought knowledge beyond the scope of an ordinary design studio, also thanks to the transdisciplinary skills and collaboration between architects, designers, artists, and engineers.

The final artifacts produced are not only an irrefutable proof of concept, but are also objects that create spatial and atmospheric experiences. Something that often gets lost in smaller-scale abstraction, but is important because "our intelligence [is] the prolongation of our senses. Before we speculate, we must live, and life demands that we make use of matter, either with our organs, which are our natural tools, or with tools properly so-called, which are artificial organs" (Bergson 1946 / 2007). By creating real-world architectural objects, we challenge our senses. The "real" affects our body in more than one dimension, like a piece of art. Simultaneously, we have to master the material constraints, digital tools, and construction techniques to create these experiences.

This brings me back to Frank and the benefits of working within his framework of *Funktionsplastik*.

Frank, my colleague, mentor, and friend, inspired me with his aptitude for thinking and realizing the impossible. I learned a lot from you and do my best to make sure that experimentation always has a place in my teaching.

References

Bergson, H. (1946) The Creative Mind: *An Introduction to Metaphysics,* Mabelle L. Andison (trans.) 2007, Citadel Press, New York, p. 43
Carl, T. (2019) *Deep Skin Architecture – Design Potential of Multi-layered Boundaries,* Springer, Wiesbaden, p. 24
Kotnik, T. (2011) "Das Experiment als Entwurfsmethode. Zur Möglichkeit der Integration naturwissenschaftlichen Arbeitens in die Architektur", in: Moravánszky, Ákos and Kerez, Christian (eds): *Experiments: Architektur zwischen Wissenschaft und Kunst.* TheorieBau, 2nd edition, Berlin, Jovis, p. 26
Pehnt W. (2004) "Lehrmeisterin Natur. Von der 'Riesenblase zum Blob' – ein architekturhistorischer Exkurs", in: *archithese* 46 / 47, p. 12
Rittel, H. (1973) "Dilemmas in a General Theory of Planning", in: *Working Papers from the Urban and Regional Development,* University of California, Berkley, p. 166
Rheinberger, H. (2014) "Über Serendipität: Forschen und Finden", in: Boehm G. et. al (eds), *Imagination: Suchen und Finden,* Paderborn, Fink, pp. 233–235
Marguin, S. et al. (2019) "Einleitung", in: Marguin et. al. (eds), *Experimentieren. Einblicke in Praktiken und Versuchsaufbauten zwischen Wissenschaft und Gestaltung,* transcript, Bielefeld, p. 9

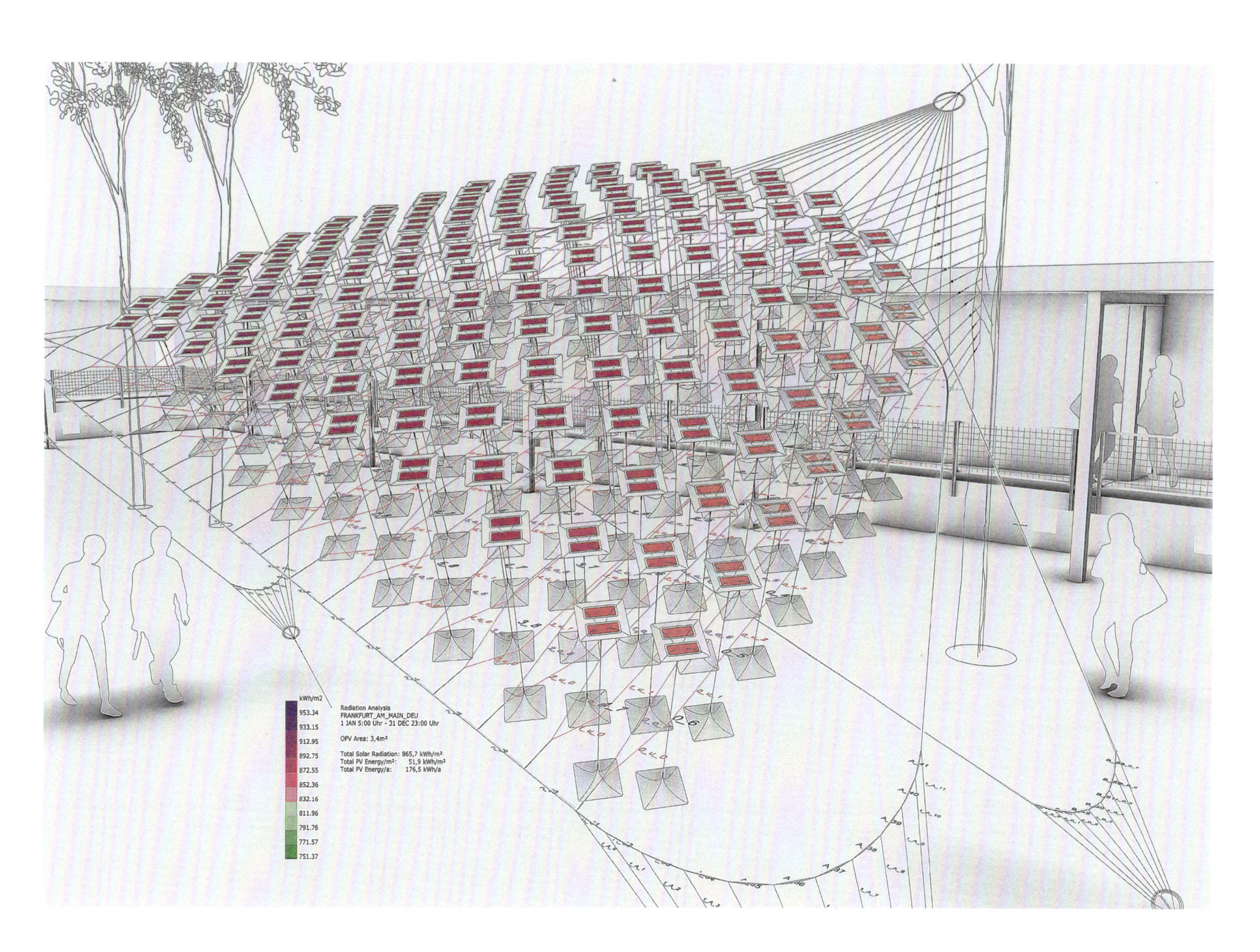
kWh/m2
953.34
933.15
912.95
892.75
872.55
852.36
832.16
811.96
791.76
771.57
751.37
Radiation Analysis
FRANKFURT_AM_MAIN_DEU
1 JAN 5:00 Uhr - 31 DEC 23:00 Uhr
OPV Area: 3,4m²
Total Solar Radiation: 865,7 kWh/m²
Total PV Energy/m²: 51,9 kWh/m²
Total PV Energy/a: 176,5 kWh/a

EXPERIMENT
↙ VIDEO

Solar Spline

In the following section, we present the design and production processes of a real world organic photovoltaic (OPV) lightweight installation realized with an interdisciplinary student team and Markus Schein from the School of Art in Kassel. The topic of this speculative design studio revolves around contemporary lightweight shading structures. Most traditional sun-sails, like the Spanish *toldos* or *velas*, are great for cooling public urban spaces. However, they do not combine their capacity for energy reflection (i.e., passive shading) with active energy generation. This simple observation sparked our research interest in inventing and building a contemporary sun-shading typology capable of harvesting energy. Furthermore, we were not interested in just adding another photovoltaic layer to the textile fabric of sun-sails, since we understood this typology as an architectural and consequently three-dimensional structure. Our goal was to redefine the traditional sun-sail typology as a modern, multi-functional solar structure with a high degree of photovoltaic integration. Additionally, we revisited Frei Otto's lightweight principles to establish design criteria based on structural and aesthetic lightness.

The result is a flexible and "fuzzy" (non-schematic) photovoltaic installation, which we named Solar Spline because the energy cloud is carried by two discrete, pre-stressed tension ropes of roughly 70 m length (d = 20 mm). Clusters of thin cables determine the shape of these two spline-like carrier rope geometries. Mapping of the sun's path in solar analysis software inspired the three-dimensional figure of these ropes. An array of thin, almost invisible dark cables (d = 2 mm) anchors the carrier ropes between a group of trees and the ground. In contrast to double curved minimal surface membranes, the linearity of our approach allows for an easy parametric model and true length measurements determined by spring particle simulations for fabrication. The tension needed to hold the structure in place is minimal compared to stand-

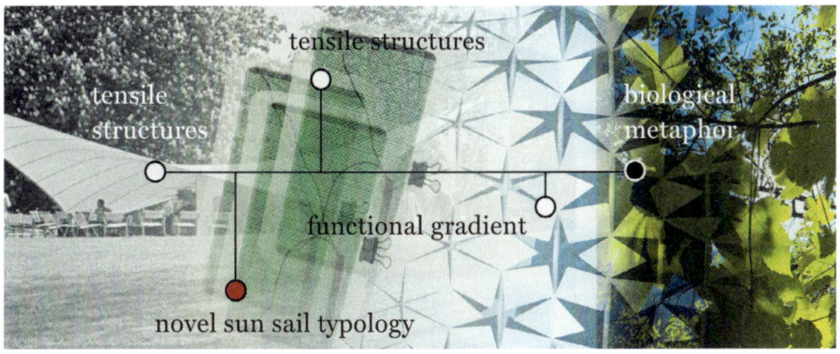

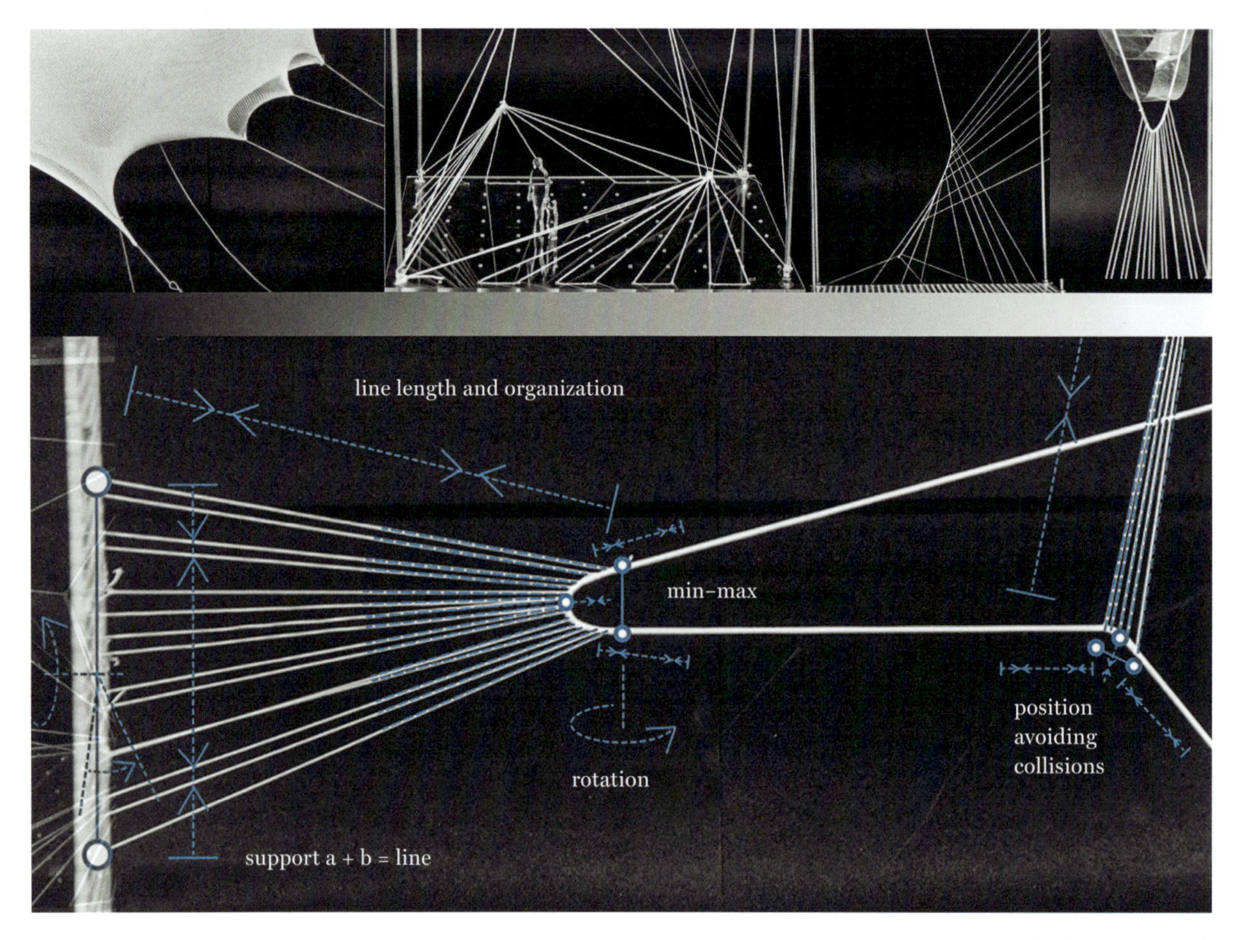

Geometric principles to control a rope in three-dimensional space and parametric model

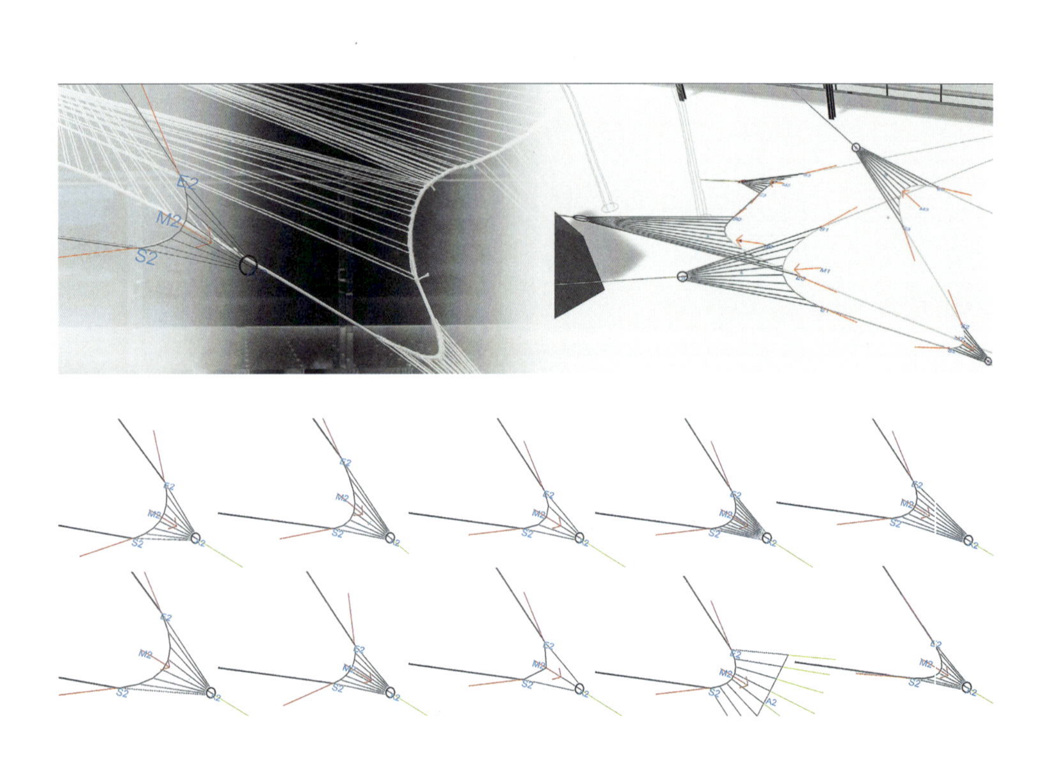

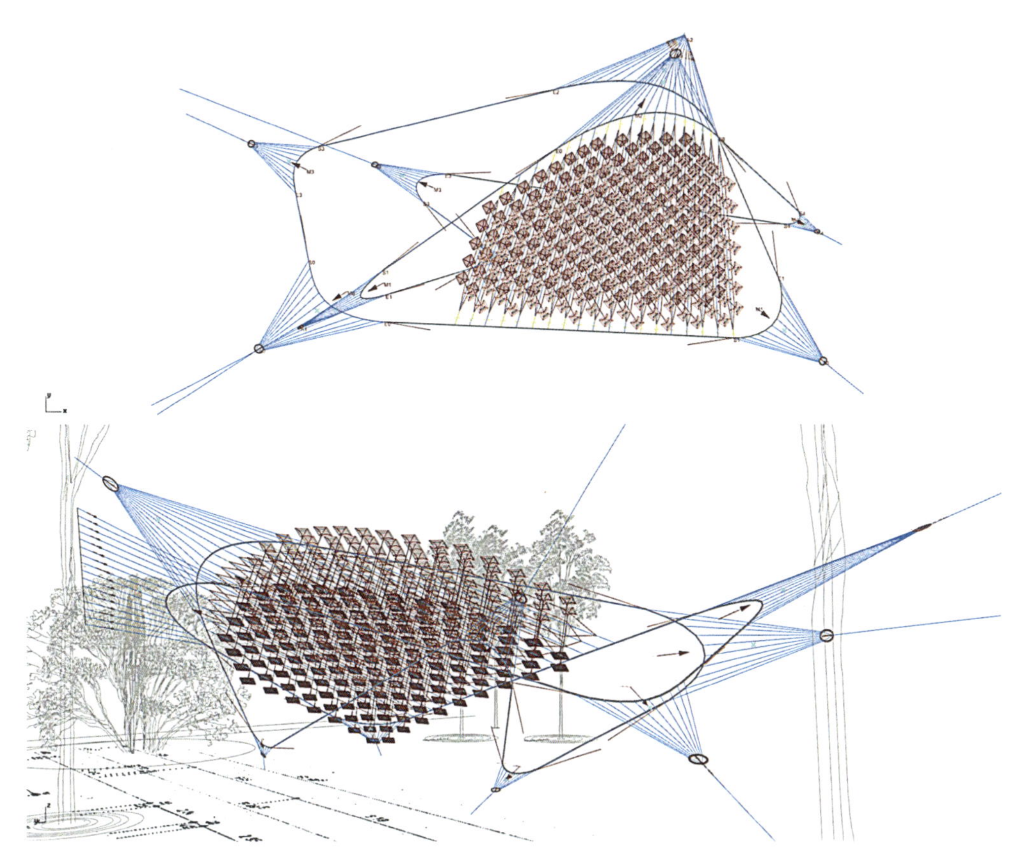

Computational form-findung
of rope geometry
under load

ard membrane structures (approx. less than 300 kg per anchor point). In consequence, the behavior of the Solar Spline corresponds more to that of a tree than to that of a textile membrane structure. Environmental forces, like wind, lead to considerable deformations (up to 50 cm) and movement, but do not damage or affect the design.

The energy cloud itself consists of 300 organic PV cells, which appear to float in midair and cover an area of about 30 m². An array of thin aluminum tubes (d = 6 mm) acts both as compression members, within a series of rope carriers, and as a mount for the thermoformed carrier panels that integrate the organic PV Modules. The overall weight, including the tensile supporting structure, is less than 120 kg.

Detail of organic PV integration

Material tests of carrier rope
Anchor point detail
Aerial view

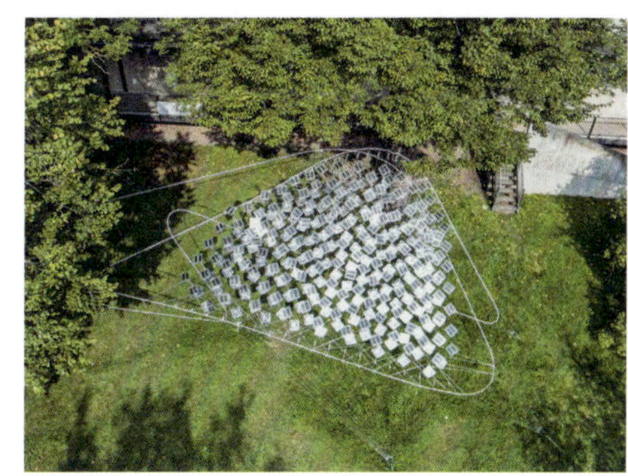

Free Skin

This project focused not only on building performance issues of external sun-shading layers, but also on their conception, which includes design and construction processes and material research with an interdisciplinary student team that included peers from computer science and engineering.

Our aim was to expand the skill-set of students by maintaining the focus on a design and build project that required a 1:1 demonstrator to test a novel lightweight construction method. Therefore, our brief encouraged students to explore secondary sun shading systems. Such systems can be retrofitted to existing buildings and constitute a supplementary layer with added functionalities. Secondary and auxiliary façade layers also correspond to the architectural idea of the Free Skin as postulated by Silvia Lavin: "The idea of the Free Skin gives new intelligence, instrumentalities and plasticity to surfaces"[1] (Lavin 2009). Our Free Skin demonstrator reduces heat loads for south facing façades by means of passive shading, while actively generating energy by implementing photovoltaic cells. Moreover, the performance of our Free Skins demonstrator unfolds during the day from the interplay of the architectural structure with the dynamic effects of sunlight and shadow and at night from intricate material effects and reactive behavior. A novel lightweight construction process, based on double curved fiber reinforced textiles with integrated photovoltaic cells and fiber optic cables expands the architectural possibilities beyond that of traditional external shading typologies.

1 Silvia Lavin, "Toward an Even Newer Architecture" in *ANY* No. 4, 2005

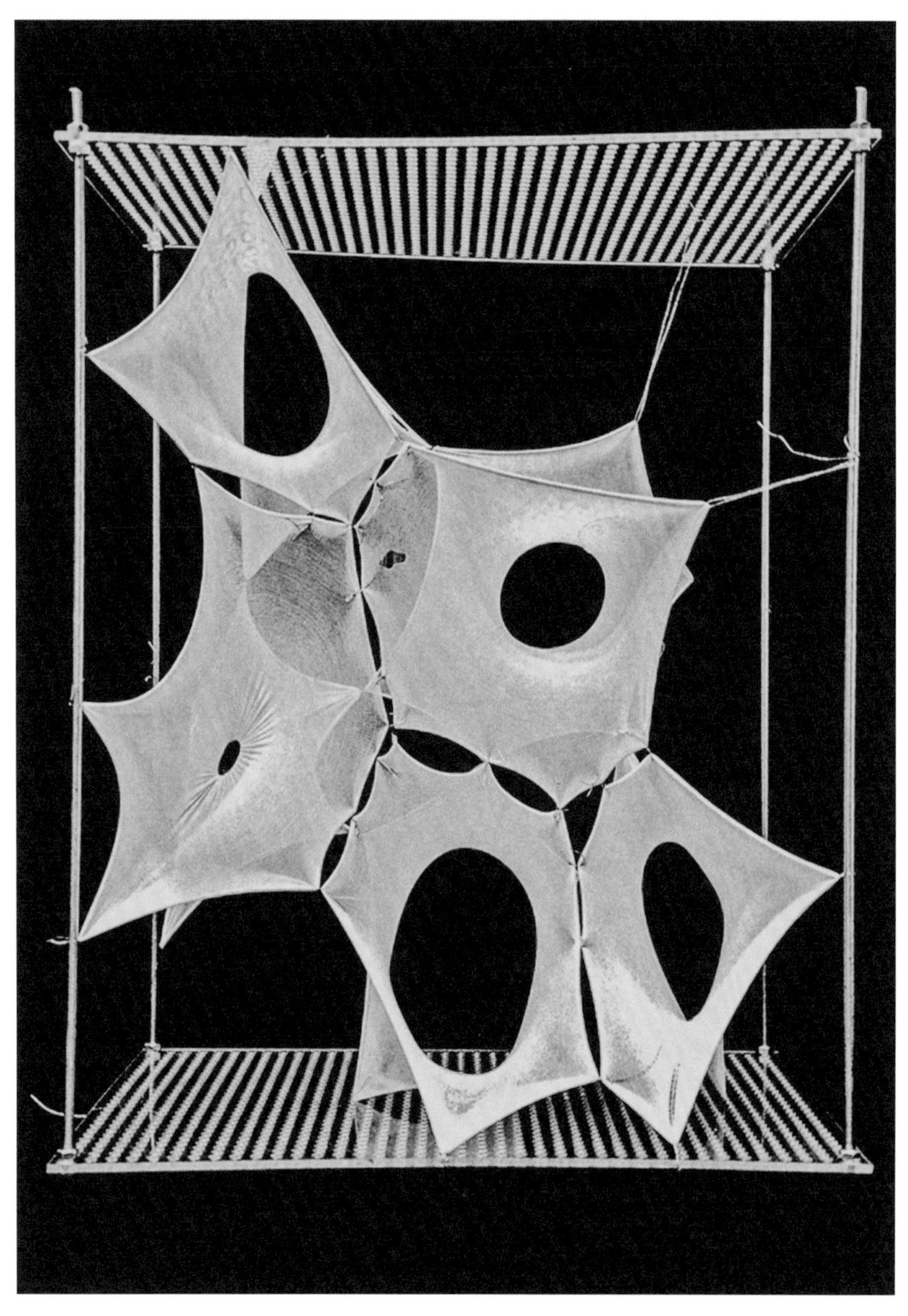

Form-finding model study

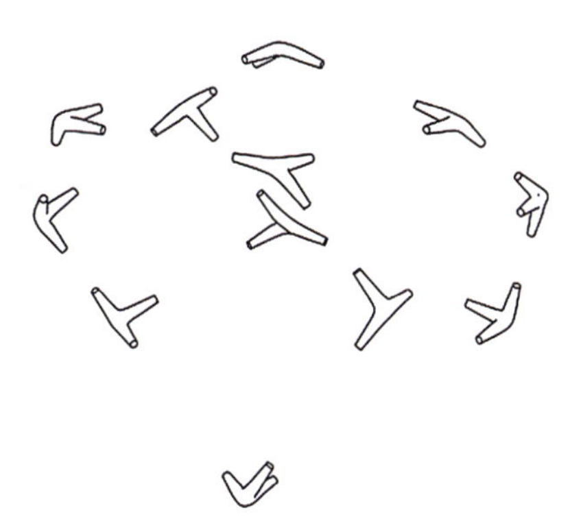

1. generation of parametric nodes

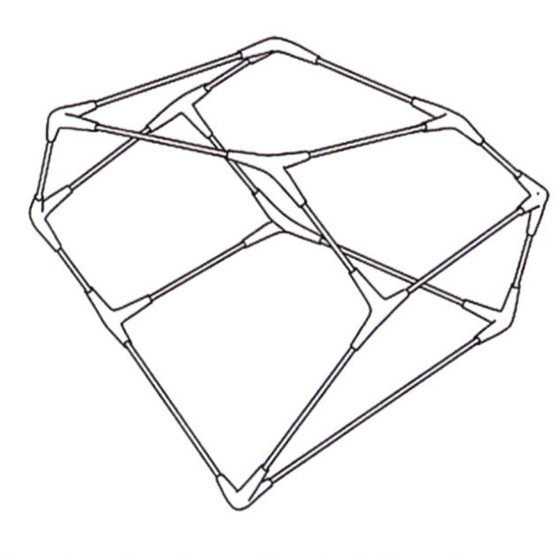

2. 3D printed nodes and rods define the geometry

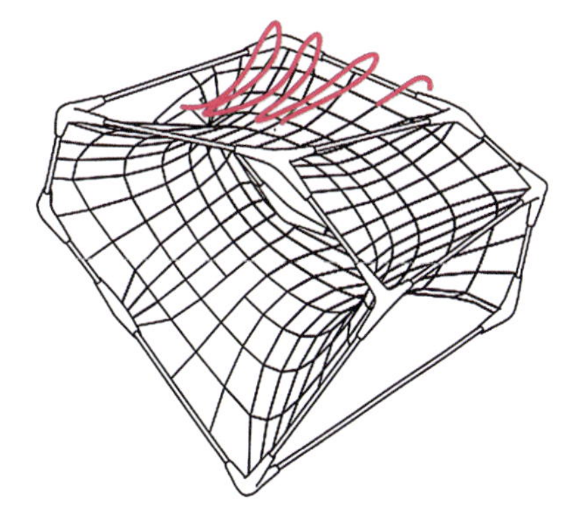

3. textile membrane acts as lost formwork

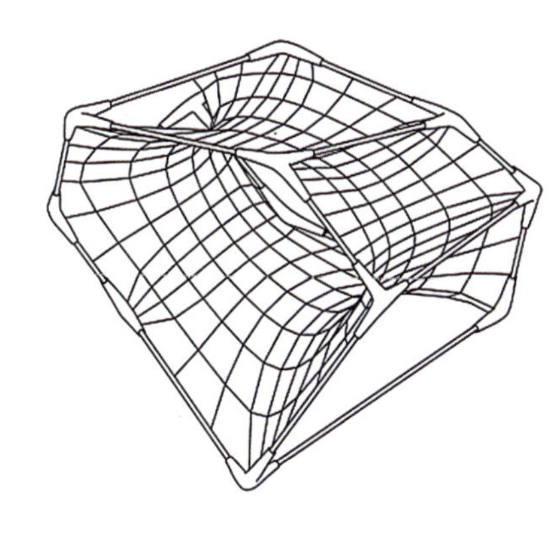

4. integration of optical fiber cables

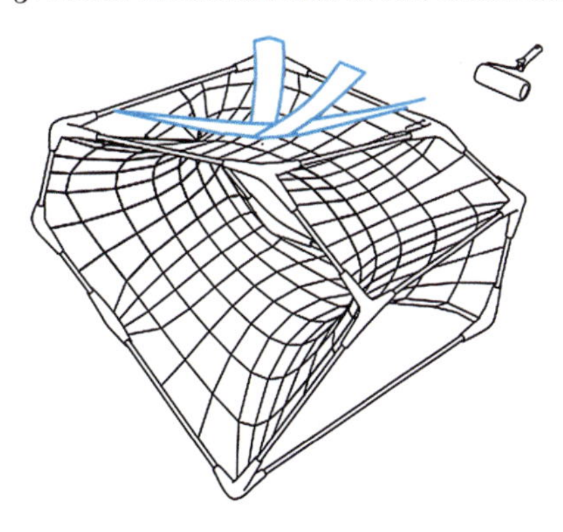

5. reinforcement with resin and local fiber mats

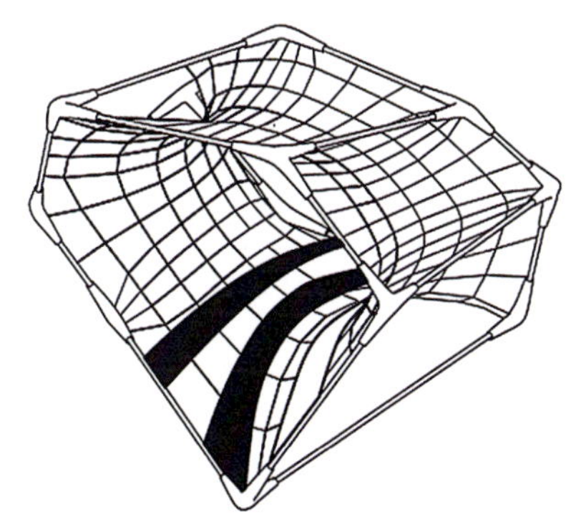

6. geometrically optimized integration of PV cells

Assembly and fabrication principle

From kit to assembled structure

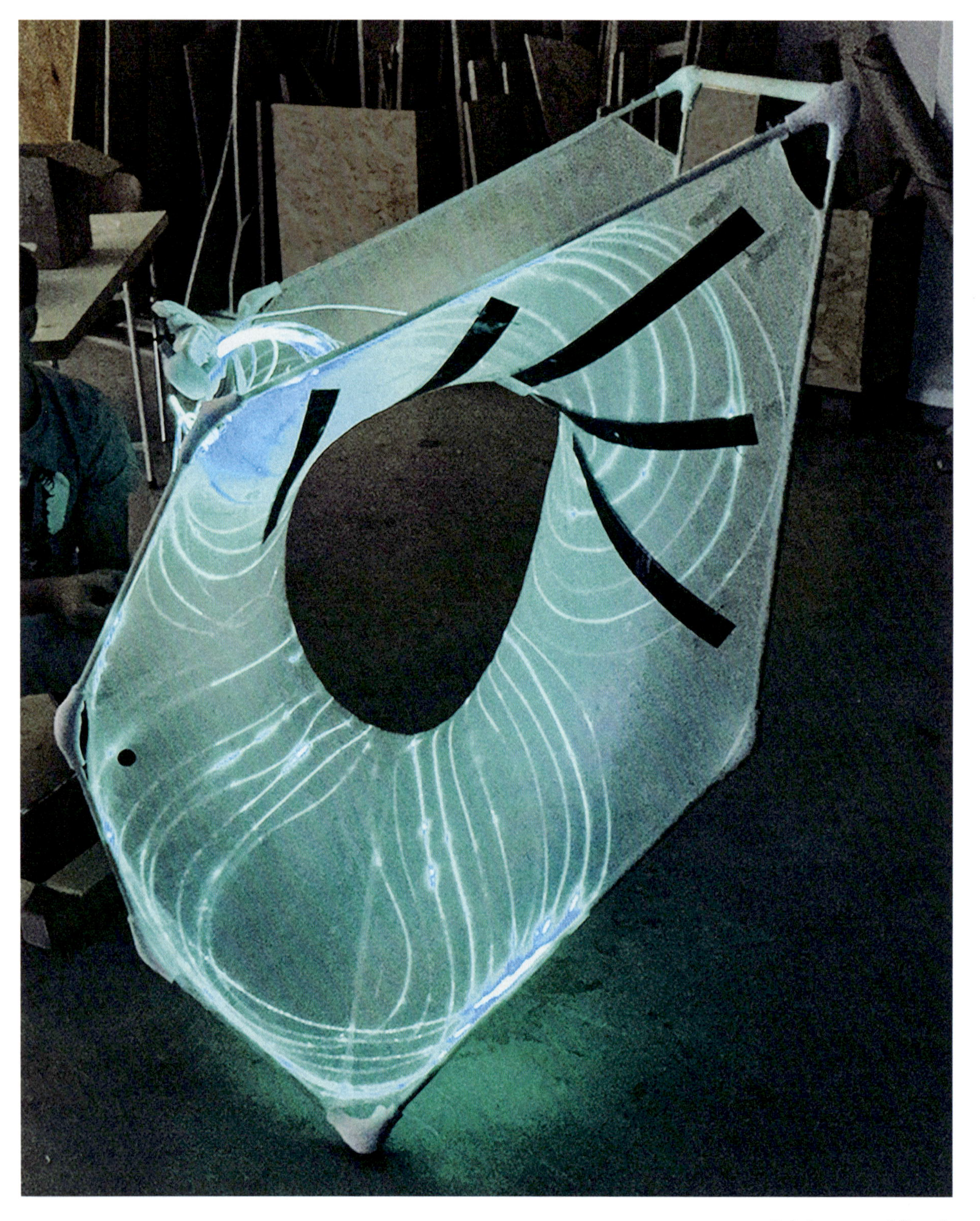

lighting test at full scale

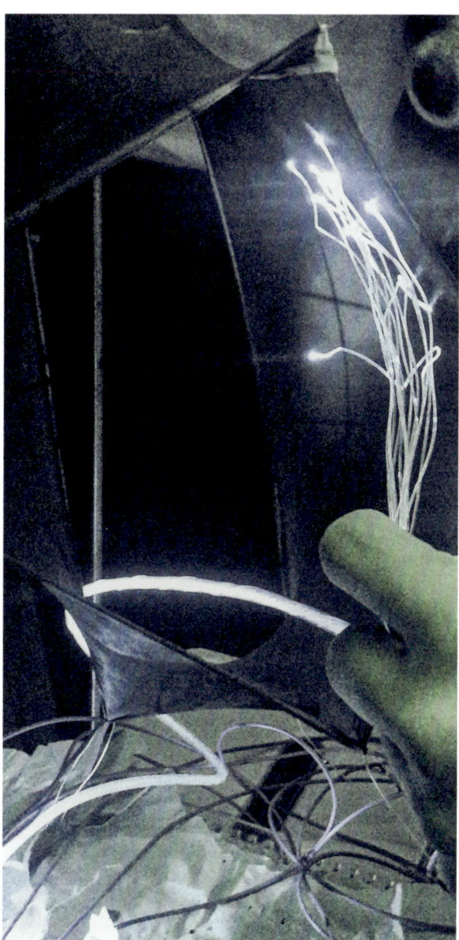

lighting experiments

Urban Glow

Walking from Kassel's city center to the outskirts of the pedestrian zone, the observer's perception shifts from a busy shopping street to a dying district with increasing vacancy in retail spaces and empty shop windows. The project, entitled Urban Glow, which operates at the interface between architecture and media-art, explores the question of how to reactivate dysfunctional urban spaces with minimal architectural interventions. This interactive implementation was developed together with the media artist Olaf Val from the School of Art, Kassel.

Together with our students, we provided a strategy for the temporary activation and interim re-use of two abandoned storefront windows with our Urban Glow installations.

Similar to acupuncture, this experiment involved the minimally invasive insertion of two performative and interactive, bio-inspired architectural creatures. Thanks to sensors and physical computing, passers-by were provided the opportunity to actively influence the behavior of these new occupants, thereby engaging with those otherwise unnoticed urban microhabitats.

In consequence, the atmosphere of the empty spaces changed substance and alternative patterns of movement and behavior emerged through an interplay of form, light, sound, and movement.

Jellyfish inspired interactive sculpture

Spectator interaction with urban glow sculpture through smart phone light

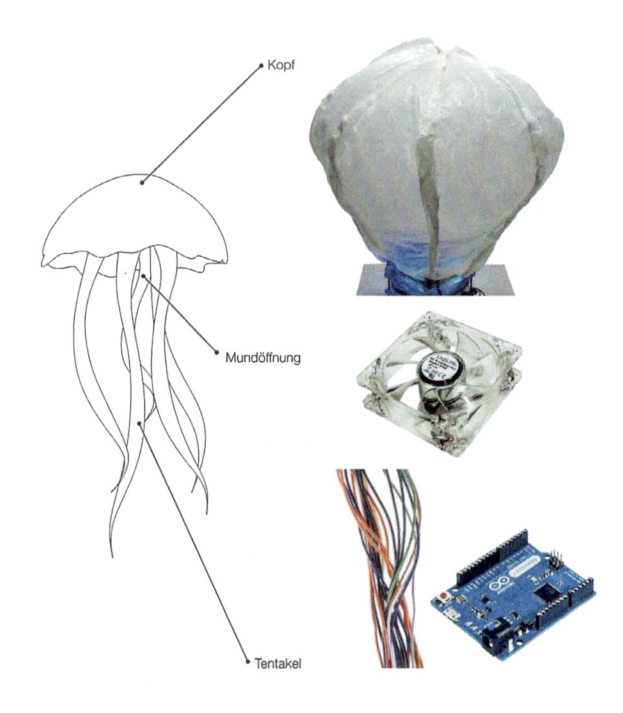

Technical jellyfish interpretation and work-in-progress during installation

Lost and Found

Lost and Found was an online seminar held at the beginning of the worldwide Covid-19 pandemic, which prevented analogue teaching for the first time. Only meeting online and unable to have physical collaboration with each other, this seminar asked students individually to focus on 2D and 3D representation techniques and translations with both digital and analogue methods of drawing and fabrication.

Deriving techniques from John Hejduk's reading of Piet Mondrian's diamond paintings[1], students applied similar operations to carefully selected and curated abstract images. The images were closely analyzed and interpreted spatially through experimenting with 2D and 3D representations. Discrete zones and spatial qualities were highlighted and described in newly formed compositions, based on their analysis and interpretations, represented in diagrams, drawings, digital, and physical models. Through iterative 2D and 3D experimental translations, using contemporary digital tools and algorithms, a feedback loop was created in the process. Students were encouraged to identify and incorporate this within their studies as they investigated spatial qualities that are Lost and Found through various translations. The goal of the seminar was to provide a deeper understanding of digital and physical methods of representing, both abstract and physical information together while enabling students to work with different digital media and fabrication methods.

1 Stan Allen, "John Hejduk's Axonometric Degree Zero," drawingmatter.org, September 23, 2019, https://drawingmatter.org/john-hejduks-axonometric-degree-zero/.

image crop / zoom in

Composition VII, Wassily Kandinsky, 1913

45° rotation and color translation

45° rotation and monochrome translation

pixelation and 3D translation

monochrome 3D translation

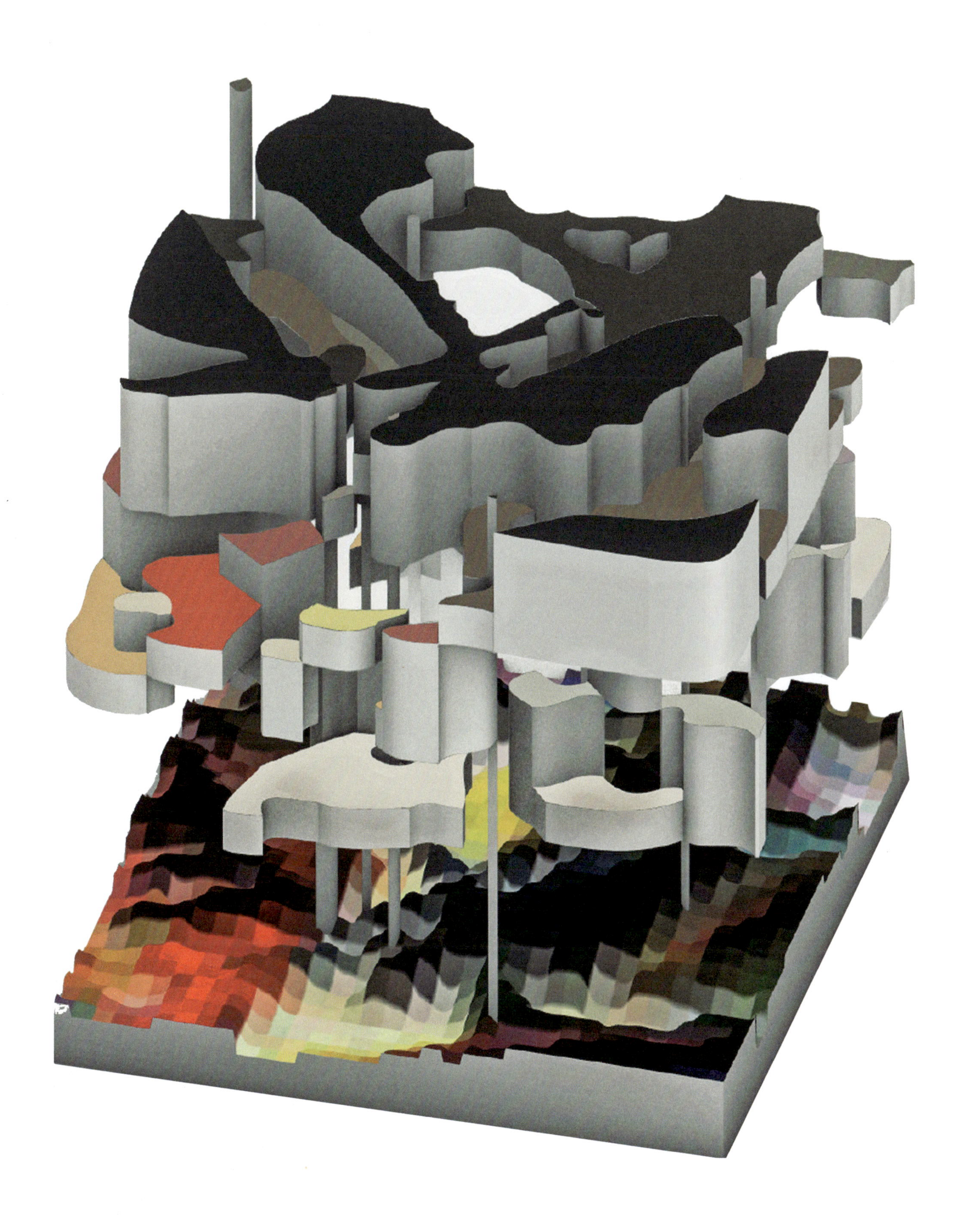

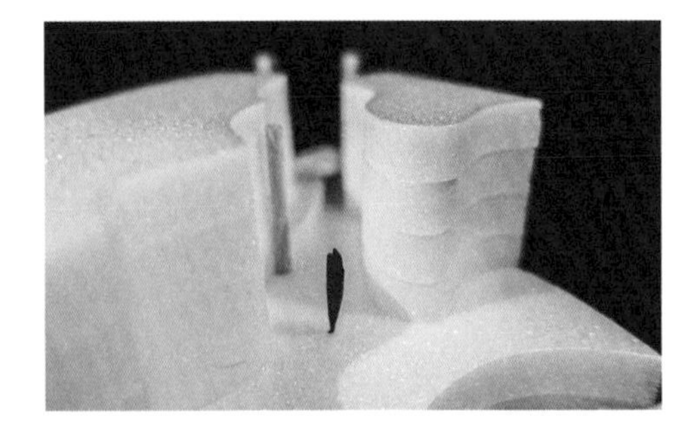

translation into physical model

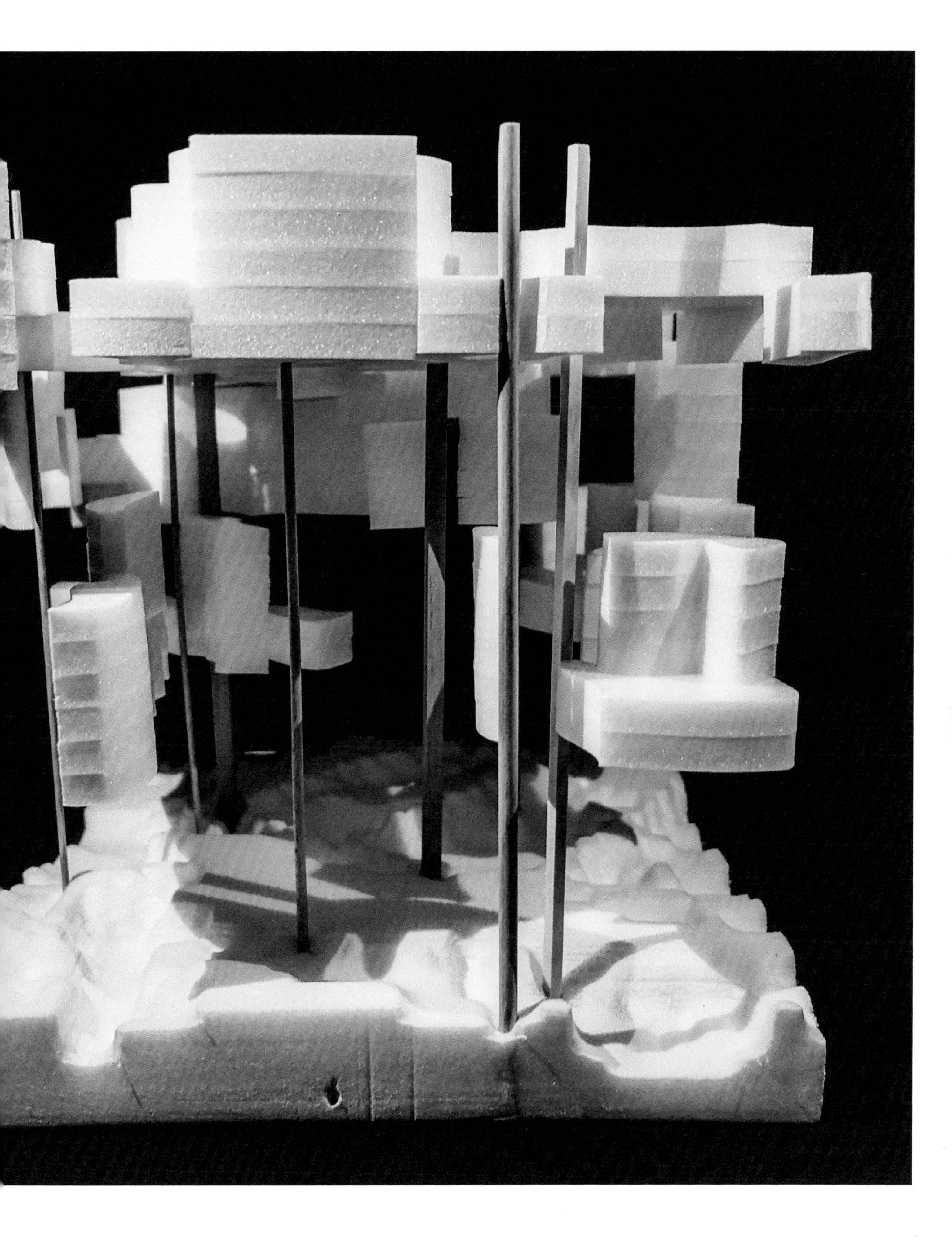

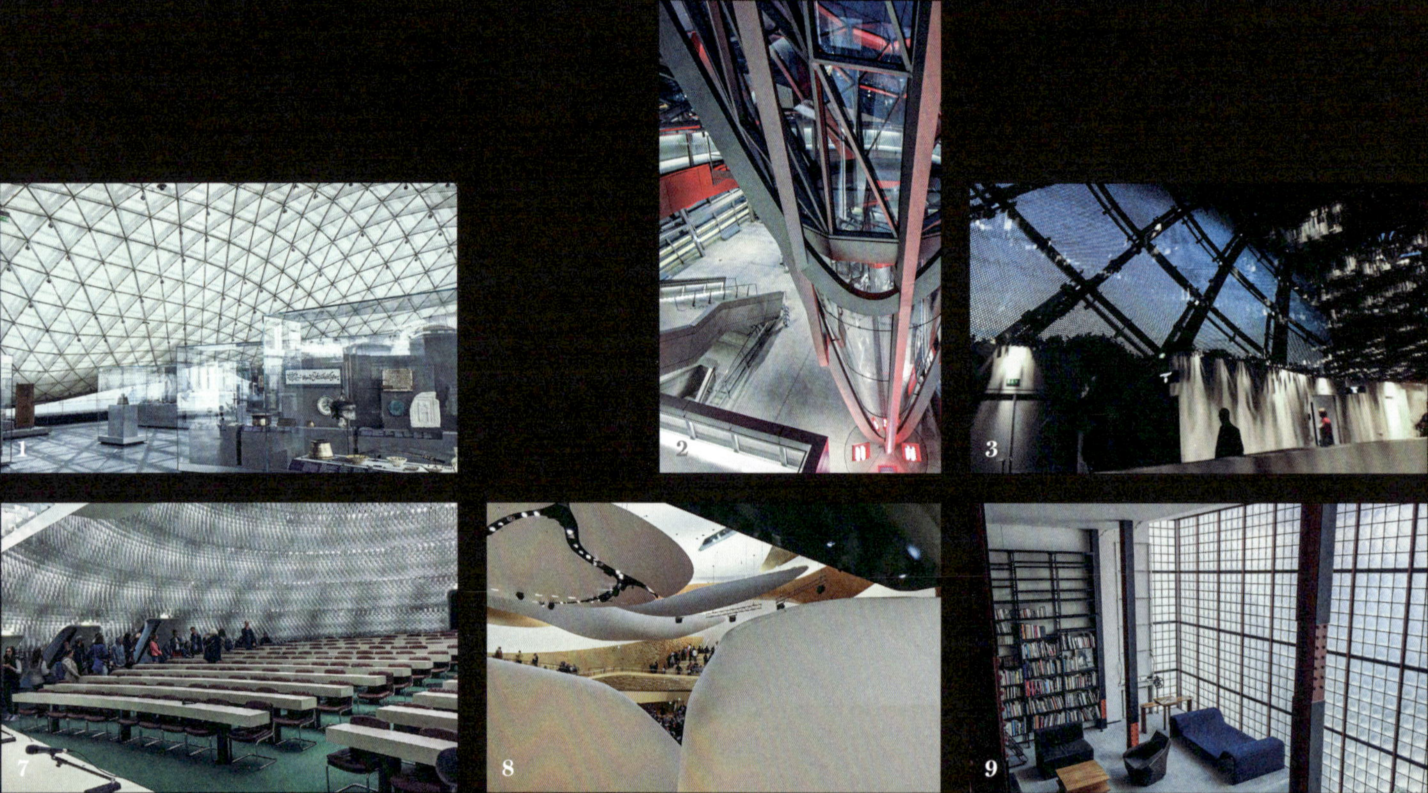
1
2
3
7
8
9

4

5

6

10

11

12

1 Louvre Extension, Rudi Ricciotti
2 Musee de Confluences, CHBL
3 Philharmonie de Paris, Jean Nouvel
4 Fondation Louis Vuitton, Frank Gehry
5 Ronchomp, Le Corbusier
6 Cite des Etoiles, Jean Renaudie
7 Communist Party HQ, Oscar Niemeyer
8 Philharmonie de Paris, Jean Nouvel
9 Maison de verre, Pierre Chareau
10 Saint Pierre Firminy, Le Corbusier
11 La Tourette, Le Corbusier
12 muCEM Marsaille, Rudy Ricciotti

In Search of Free Space in the Design Process

by Stefanie Hennecke

In Search of Free Space in the Design Process

By Stefanie Hennecke

Experimentation is the focus of Frank Stepper's teaching. Form finding is left to chance within the controlled framework of the experiment. Logic and aesthetics derived from functions – the creative and architectural principle of modernity in "form follows function" – is an approach replaced in the three thesis projects presented below by a form-finding process that results from body movement, from the explosion, or created from a computer-generated self-organization.

This approach ties in with the architectural discourses of the early 1990s, such as the subject of *Arch+* in issue no. 119 / 120: "The Architecture of the Event".[1] In his essay "The Complex and the Singular", Sanford Kwinter looks for answers in architecture to the structures of social life that are perceived as deadlocked and overly complex:

"The dominant idea is that the world ultimately consists of systems that are so massive, so dense and so complex that it is no longer a question of representing them in their totality / globality – through images, concepts, theorems or maps (all spatial models that may have become obsolete today) – but rather to support these systems at specific local points along the lines of their deployment or development. It is as if today we are forced to wage a new kind of culture war, forced to accept the mobile and changing nature of the phenomena that make up our social and political world, and thus forced to remain largely within this slippery glacis unstructured upwelling and downwelling of currents, to discover as many protruding edges, points of support, and adhesion as possible – in short: all those fine bumps that could enable us to control life in it and, as it were, to get a grip on it."[2]

When I read Kwinter's description of the situation again today, 30 years later, it still seems relevant to me. In view of the numerous problems in our world that are caused by people themselves, from climate change to massive social conditions of exploitation, which are the basis of our global economy, from the destruction of biodiversity to the collapse of infrastructure due to excessive mobility, we humans still seem to be on "slippery" reason to move. So the question remains as to how we as architects and planners want to create economically, ecologically, socially, and thus culturally viable structures in these "rising and ebbing currents". The answer to the deconstructivism of the 1990s, to which Frank Stepper, as an architect and teacher at the University of Kassel, I suspect, still ascribes himself, lay and lies in the withdrawal of one's own subjectivity as a designer. This is also shown by the three theses presented here.
The designer hands over the pen to the process. Only in the second step do they take control again and work within the process-generated material. This procedure produces impressive series of images with a fascinating variety of shapes. The scale doesn't matter at first.
The movements of a single human body, the dynamics of bending and stretching its limbs are translated into a gigantic viewing platform enclosing an aqueduct (Roda (Re)ação). A balloon filled with fine sand or a liquid is burst with a dart. What can only be perceived superficially as a process with the eye becomes a fascinating sequence through the targeted selection of individual images from a film recording, the formal language of which can serve as a model for building designs (explosion spaces). And a computing process controlled by an algorithm in a computer produces self-generating and changing forms that can be interpreted

as an adequate basis for the new construction of Kowloon Walled City. It is interesting that the basis for the growth algorithm was a set of social rules. The implementation of investors' interest in high profits was linked to the provision of social infrastructure and translated into a volume unit rather than an area unit. The form-finding processes of the three works presented in this chapter are neither about a rational derivation from the context on site, nor about direct analogy between the inspiring experiments and the object developed from them. Rather, it is about translating the dynamics of a movement in time into a form that is permanently effective in space.

This approach favors "emergence" over "planned". It refuses the rational. This is consistent when one questions the rationality of planning, when one assumes that the idea that one can develop the "optimal" solution to a problem must always remain an illusion. In view of the challenges to human society in 2023 listed above, this illusion can be formulated even further: The claim to plan an optimum always has authoritarian and destructive traits. Planning is never innocent but represents interests. With the assertion of interests, the living conditions of other people are always impaired, changed, or even destroyed.

Leaving the finding of form to chance to a certain extent shows a way of refusing rational planning without having to refrain from building itself. The non-smooth, non-optimal form offers points of contact for chance itself, as life generates it every second. The form, which is not consciously designed, can trigger unplanned processes, offer space for unplanned uses, can develop niches and protuberances, rashes and dynamics, just as the complexity of societies produces at any time. The architecture studio Coop Himmelb(l)au of architect Wolf D. Prix, to which Frank Stepper also belonged, formulated its concept of "open architecture" in a very similar way in 1991: "For us, 'open architecture' is architecture that is initially intended without dedication, self-confident structures, that form differentiated spaces. Spaces that do not define the future user, but confidently offer them opportunities."[3]

In a book that I published with Annette Geiger and Christin Kempf in 2005, we reflected on the varieties of the organic in architecture, design, and art and classified the deconstructivist claim to design as a variant of organic architecture that does not rely on the existence of a higher harmony:

"People and their interests, and thus also the artist as creator, have to recede into the background in order to perceive themselves as part of a higher entity. This can be conceived as a harmonious whole or as infinite, chaotic abundance and changeability – in any case, it should always mean a departure from the usual perspectives, that is, it dedifferentiates dualisms and binaries on a higher level of consideration. In doing so, the individual has to withdraw completely from their 'egoistic' demands. Above all, this decidedly anti-anthropocentric attitude criticizes the idealistic conception of modernity that human beings are by nature open to progress, rational, autonomous individuals."[4]

The three theses show studies in which the designers consciously withdraw from the design process in order to eliminate their own experience, conception of norms, and conventions from the design: "To do this, however, the architect has to outwit themself, because ultimately they (as a subject) is not able to create a new image free of metaphors without the unconscious influence of their own clichés and images."[5]

This outwitting of one's own creative will can be seen in the experiment with the exploding balloon and the study of the diverse forms that emerge from the photos of the repeated iterations of the experiment. The camera, or in the case of the design for Kowloon Walled City, the computer, are completely neutral in relation to the forms that are technically generated here:

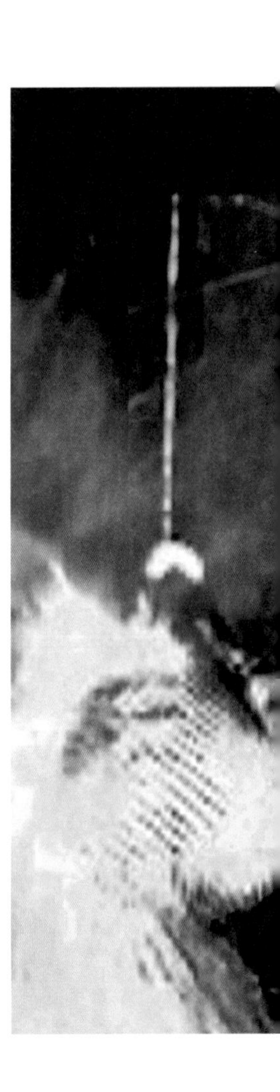

"Due to the innocence of the machine (after all, it is completely 'naive' in terms of morality, tradition and convention) the designer hopes to stumble upon images that they themself would have rationally ruled out in the creation process, or that they would not have been able to develop due to their extreme complexity."[6] Architect Stan Allen pointed out that the search for form in the event is not a completely undirected process, but rather the exploration of potential areas within the framework of a controlled experimental setup according to scientific standards. He describes the result of the exploration process as a "diagram": "A diagram is therefore not a thing in itself, but a description of potential relationships among elements, not only an abstract model of the way things behave in the world, but a map of possible worlds."[7] This deconstructive approach refers to the book *A Thousand Plateaus* by Giles Deleuze and Felix Guatari, which has been widely read in this context: "The diagrammatic or abstract machine does not function to represent, even something real, but rather construct a real that is yet to come, a new type of reality".[8]

I also recognize the search for the infinite and diagrammatic abundance of forms as a source of inspiration in the three thesis projects presented here, supervised by Frank Stepper and Timo Carl. All three projects choose very individual approaches. They tap into the natural processes in very different ways, so to speak. And the resulting architectural spaces refuse a simple logic of use, just as their predecessors refused in the 1990s: "The 'new' architecture, as propagated by the deconstructivists, becomes an expression of arbitrariness. Unpredictability, defiant and fleeting, emancipated from conservative homeliness and unwieldy in relation to old-fashioned usage habits. People should not make any use of this philosophically exaggerated architecture; rather, they should be educated to deal creatively with the space in front of them."[9]

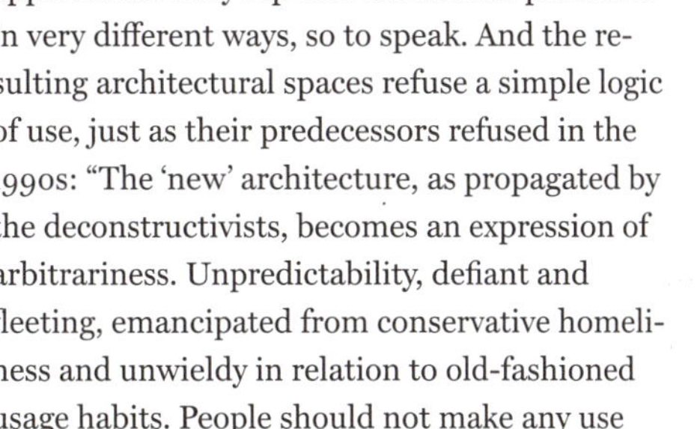

In open space planning, we have long addressed the creative handling of spatial planning under the concept of appropriation. We observe, describe, and analyze how people deal with planned spaces, how they often take possession and creatively reinterpret them despite and not because of the planning specifications: "After its first peak in the planning theory of the 1960s and 1970s, the concept of appropriation becomes recently taken up again in discourses on the theory, practice and politics of urban development. In view of the dynamics of late modern economy and politics, which are perceived as inescapable, it is all about the availability and self-determined use of space and quality in everyday life, accompanied by buzzwords such as 'deceleration', 'do-it-yourself' or 'sharing'."[10] Whether and how the appropriation of deconstructivist architectures can work remains unanswered here. The cooperation in teaching and in council between departments for open space planning and experimental design in any case worked very well and in a friendly way.

1 The Architecture of the Event, *Arch+*, Issue 119 / 129, December 1993, Berlin.
2 Sanford Kwinter, "The Complex and the Singular," The Architecture of the Event, *Arch+*, Issue 119 / 129, December 1993, Berlin, 79.
3 Wolf Prix 1991, quoted in Christin Kempf, "Das Prinzip Unschuld – Computergeneriertes Entwerfen und die neue Organik in der Architektur," in *Spielarten Des Organischen in Architektur, Design Und Kunst.* (Berlin: Reimer, 2005), 187.
4 Annette Geiger, Stefanie Hennecke, and Christin Kempf, *Spielarten Des Organischen in Architektur, Design und Kunst* (Berlin: Reimer, 2005), 11.
5 Kempf, "Das Prinzip," 189.
6 Ibid.
7 Stan Allen, "Diagrams Matter" in *ANY* No. 23, 1988 (I thank Timo Carl for this reference and also the following one to Deleuze and Guatari).
8 Gilles Deleuze et al., *A Thousand Plateaus: Capitalism and Schizophrenia* (Minneapolis; London: University of Minnesota Press, 2014), https://www.bibliovault.org/BV.book.epl?ISBN=9780816614028.
9 Kempf, "Das Prinzip," 187.
10 Thomas E Hauck, Stefanie Hennecke, and Stefan Körner, *Aneignung Urbaner Freiräume* (Transcript Verlag, 2017), 7.

Roda (Re)ação

MA Thesis: Roda (Re)ação, 2012
by Ernesto M. Mulch, Stefan Niggemeyer

Roda (Re)ação is a space, a mood, a feeling. It is a functional sculpture, sustainably designed, widely accessible, and versatile. Inspired by Capoeira, a Brazilian art form that combines dance, martial arts, and music, Roda (Re)ação interprets the flowing movements of the Capoeiristas into a sculptural figure that is both plastic and medial. Roda (Re)ação embodies our idea of kinetic, flexible, ever evolving architecture, capable of adapting to the situational demands and needs of the users. In Capoeira, Roda describes the circle formed by the Capoeiristas and the musicians – the place of Lapa as Roda represents the spatial part of our design. The arches of the aqueduct, Arcos da Lapa embody the imaginary line between the Capoeiristas, who shall never touch while dancing in Roda.

For the sculptural part of our design – (Re)ação – we translate the Capoeiristas into a functional landscape on one side and a medial façade on the other side – two dancing media roofs. Like Capoeiristas, the kinetic sculptures react to each other, complement each other, dance with each other. According to the variety of movements in Capoeira, the roofs can adapt to diverse requirements, such as public screenings, concerts, or fashion shows. Set up vertically the roofs create an observation deck and at the same time provide screens for an open-air cinema on the outside. When not in use, they create an extension of the urban space.

old and new: aqueduct and superstructure

EXPERIMENT
↙ VIDEO

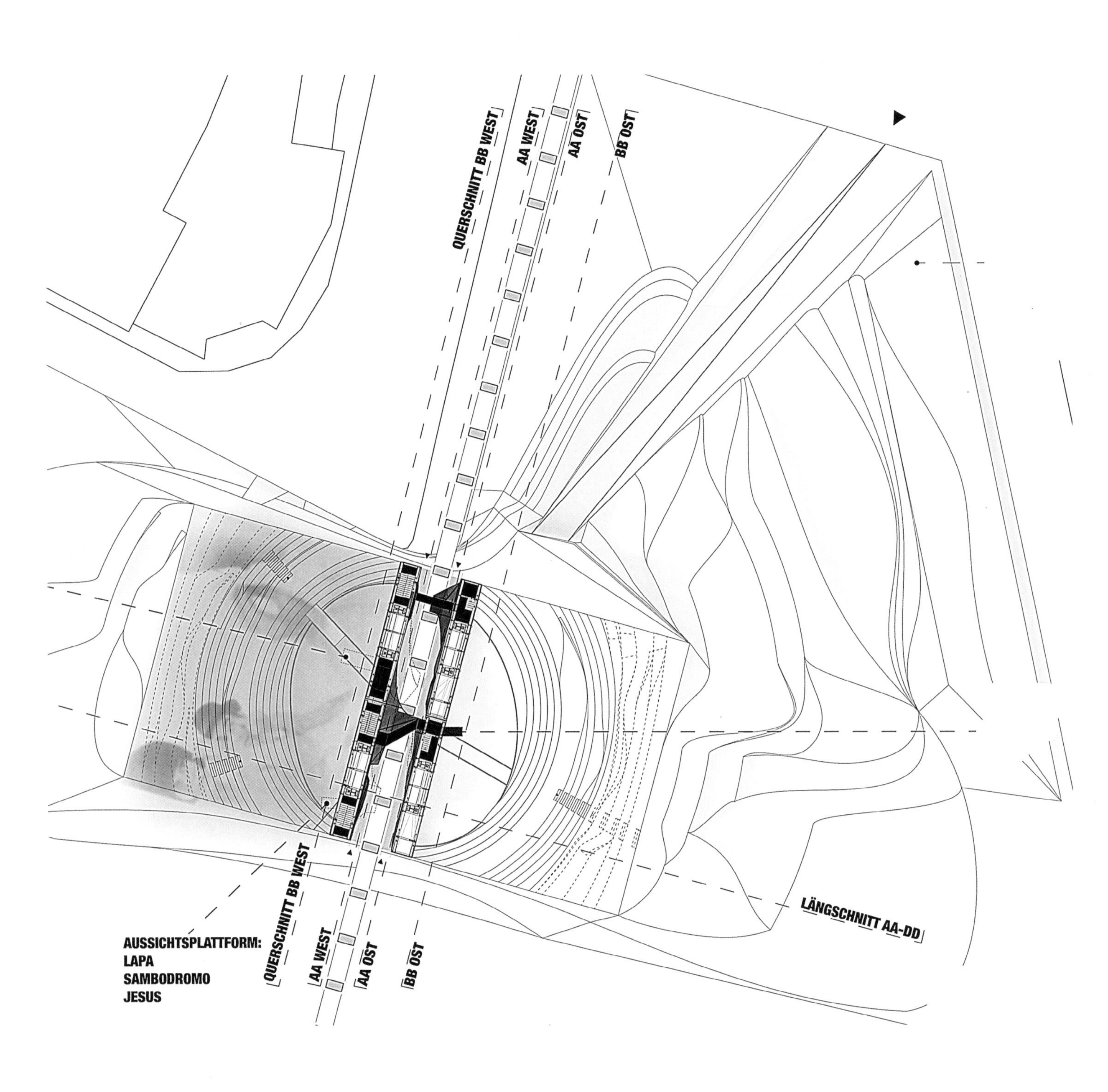

movement analysis of Capoeira

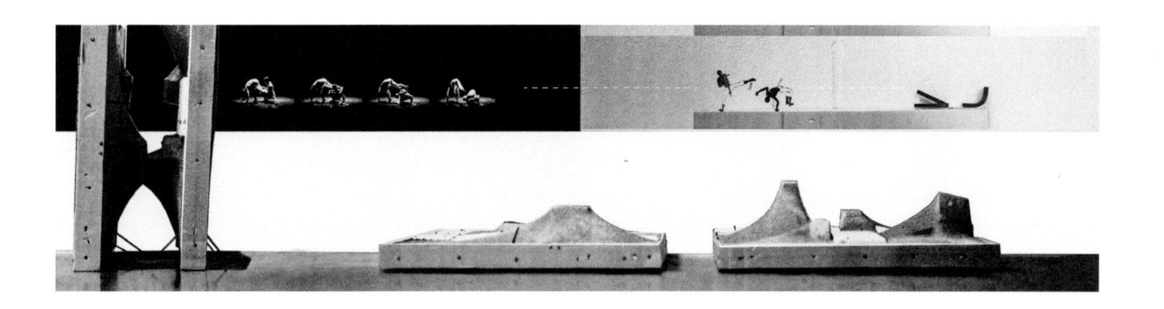

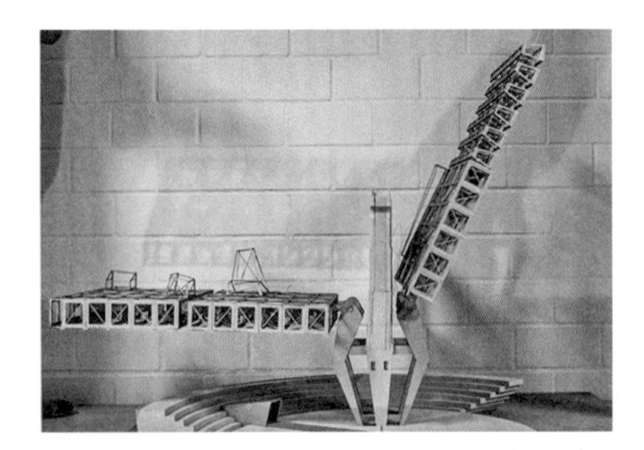

transformation of structure and functions

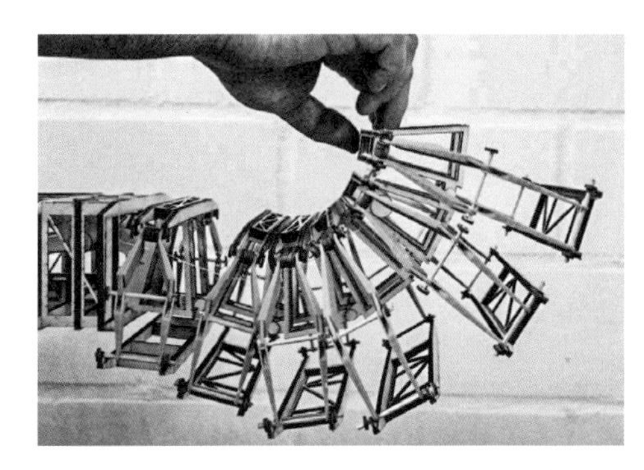

movement studies

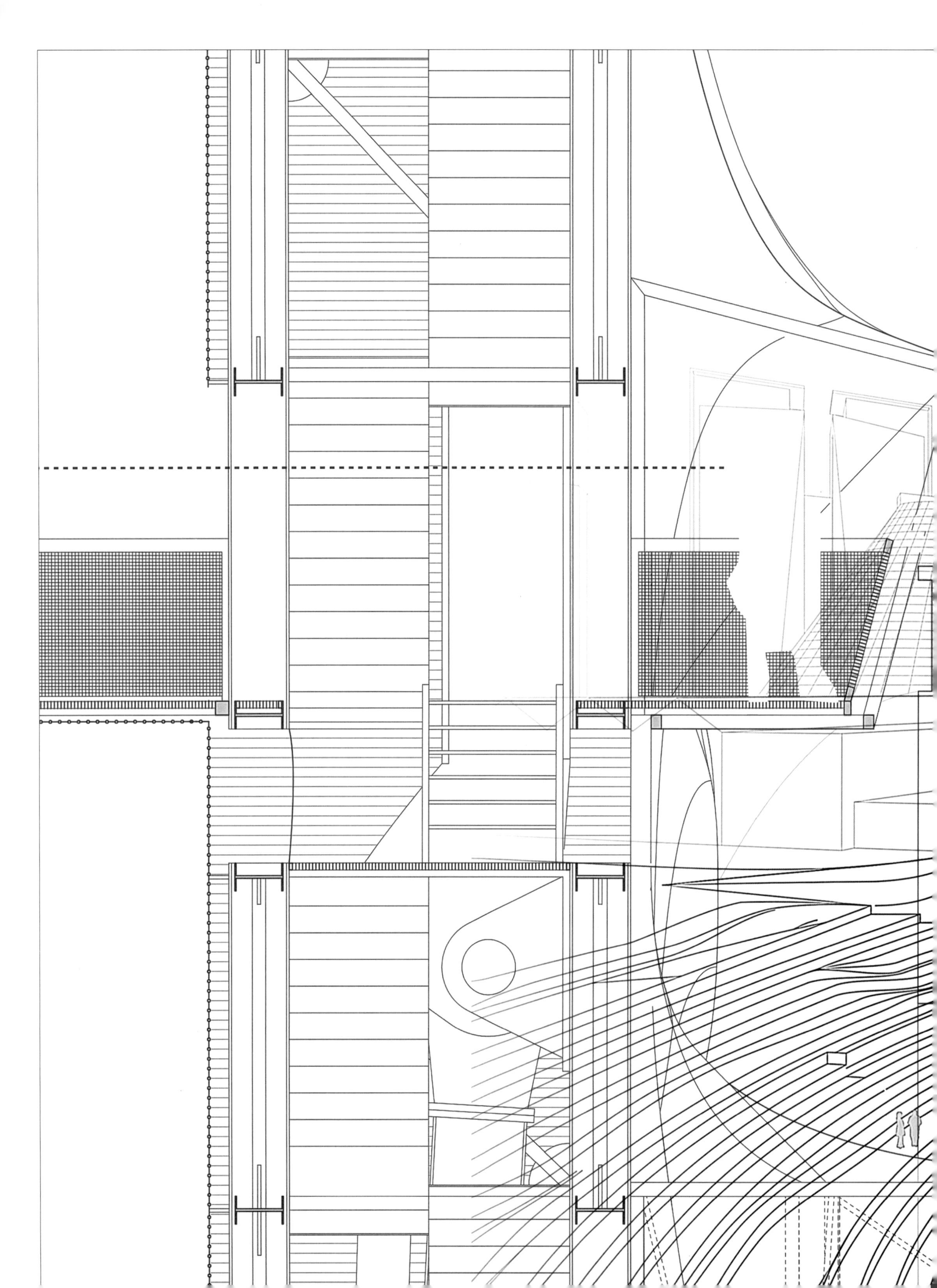

movement, space, and atmosphere

BA Thesis: Explosionsräume, 2018
by Sarah Metwally, Eugenia Schlag
"Explosion Spaces" – mesh and latex envelopes with powder

Explosionsräume

With the topic "explosion space", question is how do variations influence the parameters of the explosion chambers and their spatial distribution if the same conditions exist? The initial experiment is analyzed and further developed with regard to its parameters. The aim is to find out the extent to which the different materials affect the quality of the result.

Various extensions of experiments are listed and analyzed for this purpose. In order to be able to examine the test phases in the same way, each experiment is presented in a stereometric series of images and provided with a number of seconds, through which exactly the same moments can be compared with one another. Furthermore, each experiment is evaluated by means of a textual, as well as a diagrammatic analysis.

The experiments all have the same process and main components and are therefore exposed to the same basic requirements. The components are a reaction trigger, a membrane, and an explosive. An additional part of the work is generating and printing a 3D model of one of the experiments. The 3D model and print of the chosen experiment were extracted from an actual simulation of the experiment via 3D software and then adjusted to be printable. The model is used for the spatial representation of the experiment and a haptic recording.

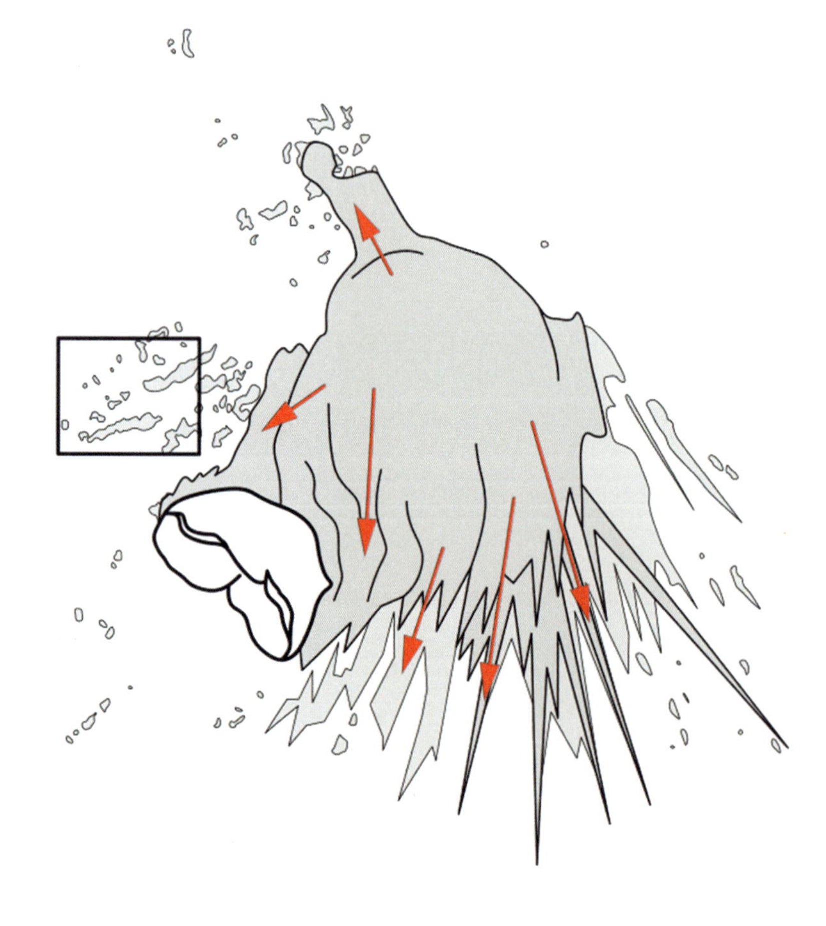

reaction triggers:
dart + mesh envelope + powder
dart + latex membrane + powder

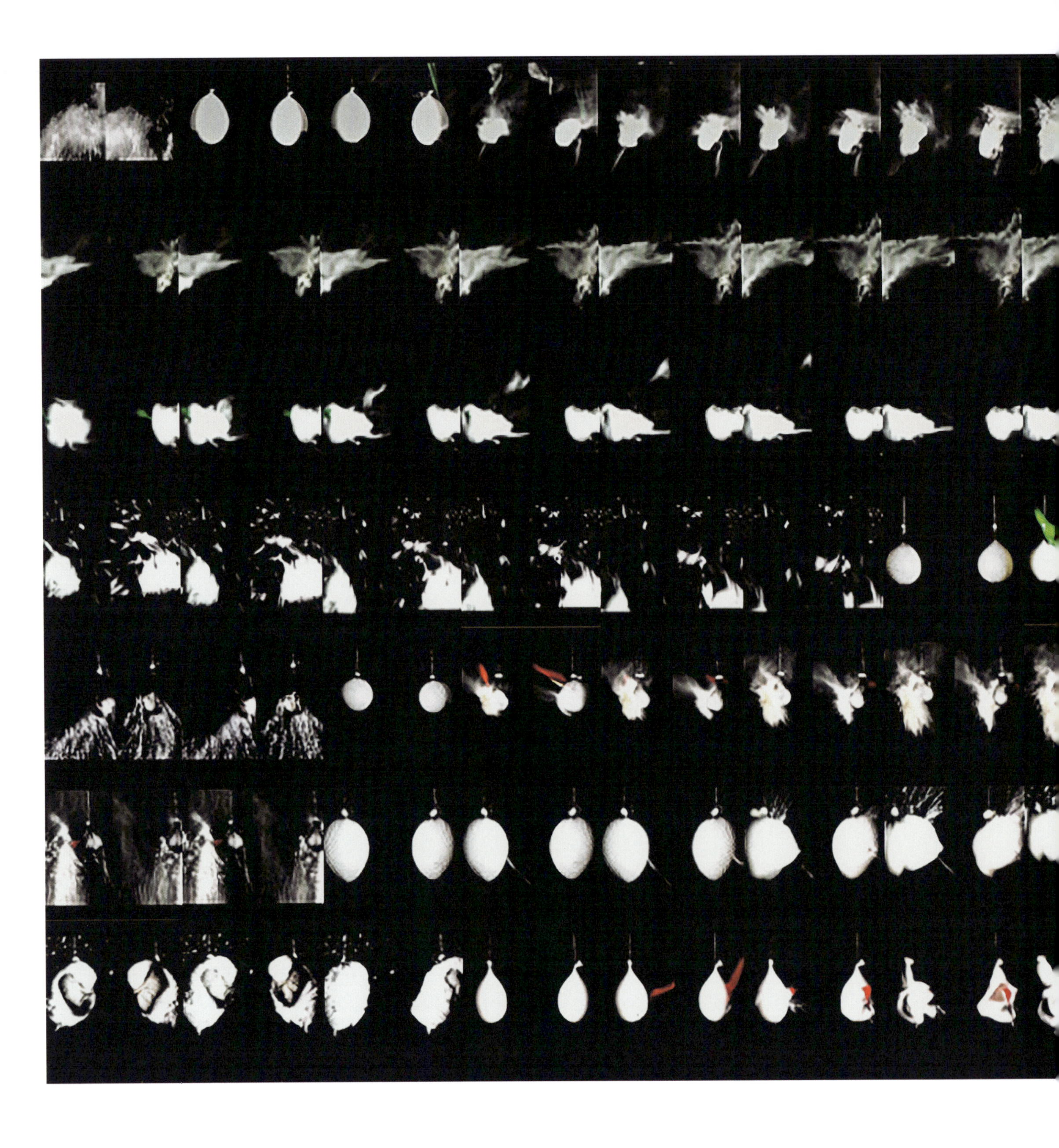

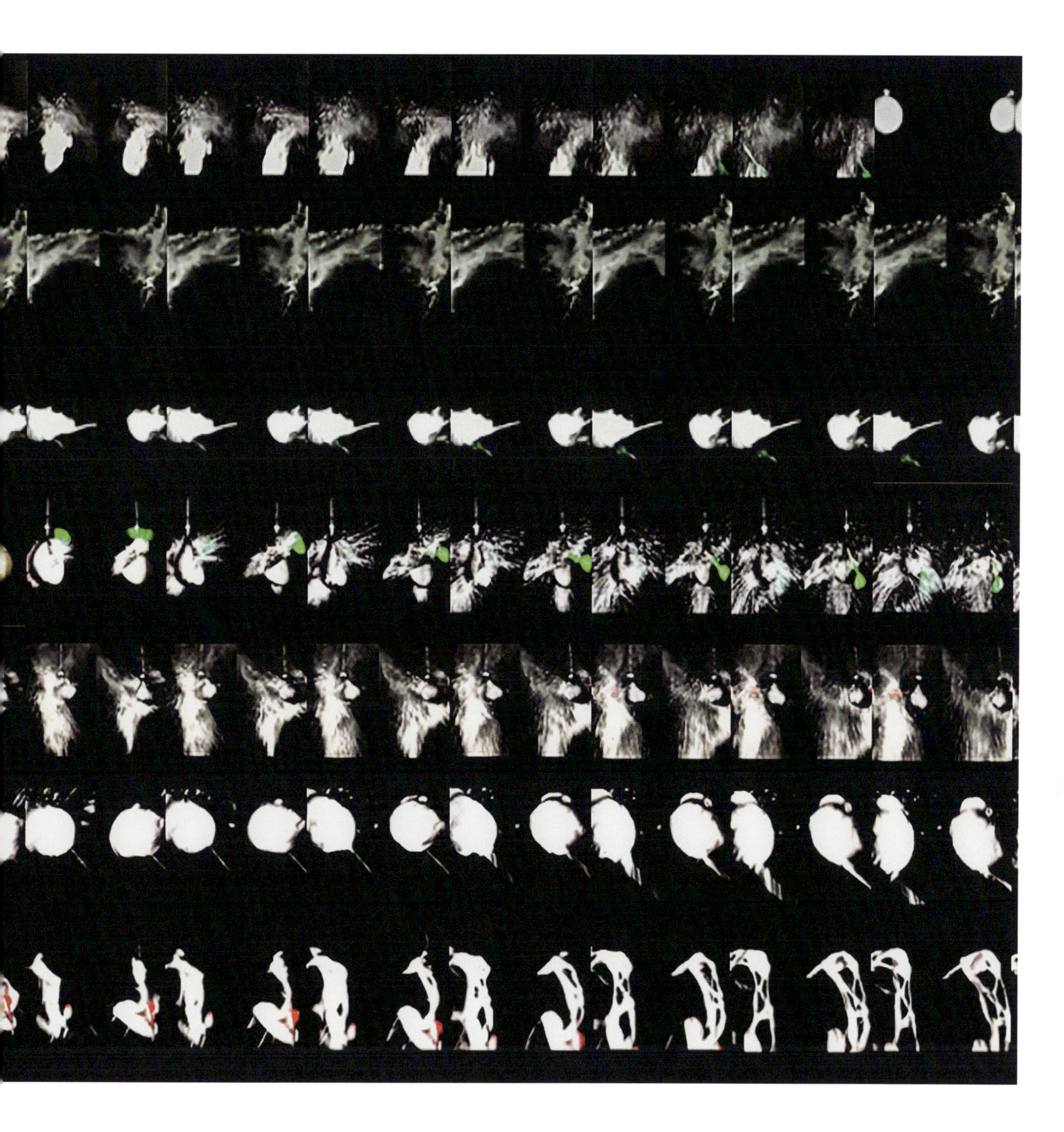

Kowloon Walled City – 3D Urban Planning

As the title suggests, this thesis investigates the vision of the "rebirth" of Hong Kong's infamous, ungoverned, and densely populated Kowloon Walled City.

Within the scope of a futuristic utopia, in which the air space above the former international airport becomes available for three-dimensional urban growth, the new city abandons the ground and rises into the sky, following the long evolving volumetric character of Hong Kong. This spatial emergence is to be shaped by spatial urban planning regulations, which aim to guarantee the basic principles of light, air, sun, and space – all which the former "city of darkness" fundamentally lacked.

Rules that regulate density, polycentricity, multifunctionality, investment policies, mobility, and infrastructure are the DNA (Deoxyribonucleic acid) that creates a volumetric urban plan.

A 3D plot plan, as well as the digitally simulated population thereof was created by using a flocking particle network that followed a representation of bespoke rules.

The simulation mirrors the regulated growing and shrinking behavior of the city over a set timeline.

Inspired by the social harmony of the inhabitants of the former city despite the inhumane conditions they lived in, how would the new city achieve a high level of social cohesion while simultaneously guaranteeing quality of life?

In this regard, it was crucial to set a framework for the latter without interfering with a self-evolving city while leaving plenty of scope for informalities, diversity, and organic growth.

"It cannot be planned, it can only happen."[1]
Yona Friedman

1 Friedman Yona: *Pro Domo.* (Barcelona: Actar, 2006), 234.

MA Thesis: Kowloon Walled City – 3D Urban Planning,
by Ricardo Valencia Paez

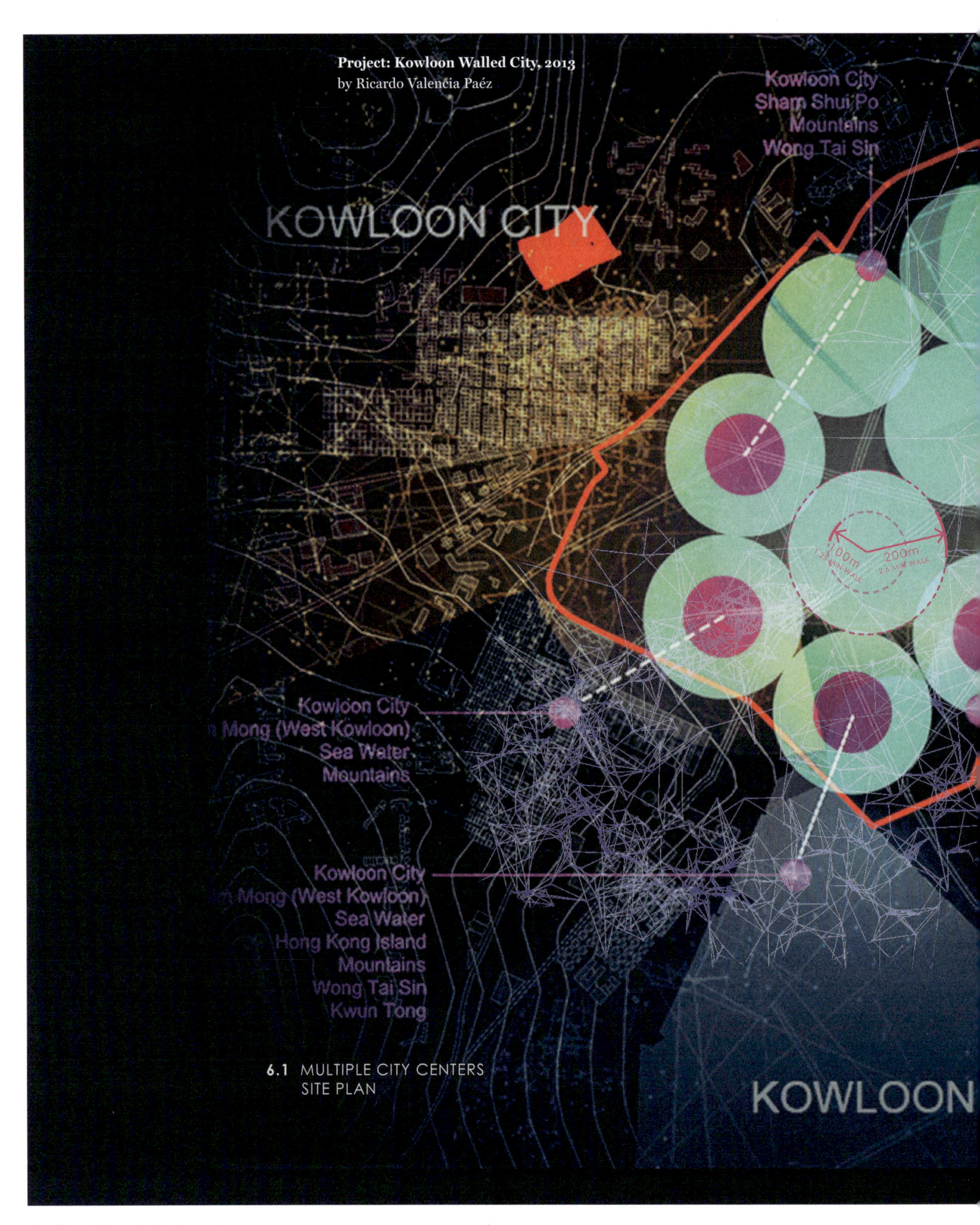

site plan with multiple city centers

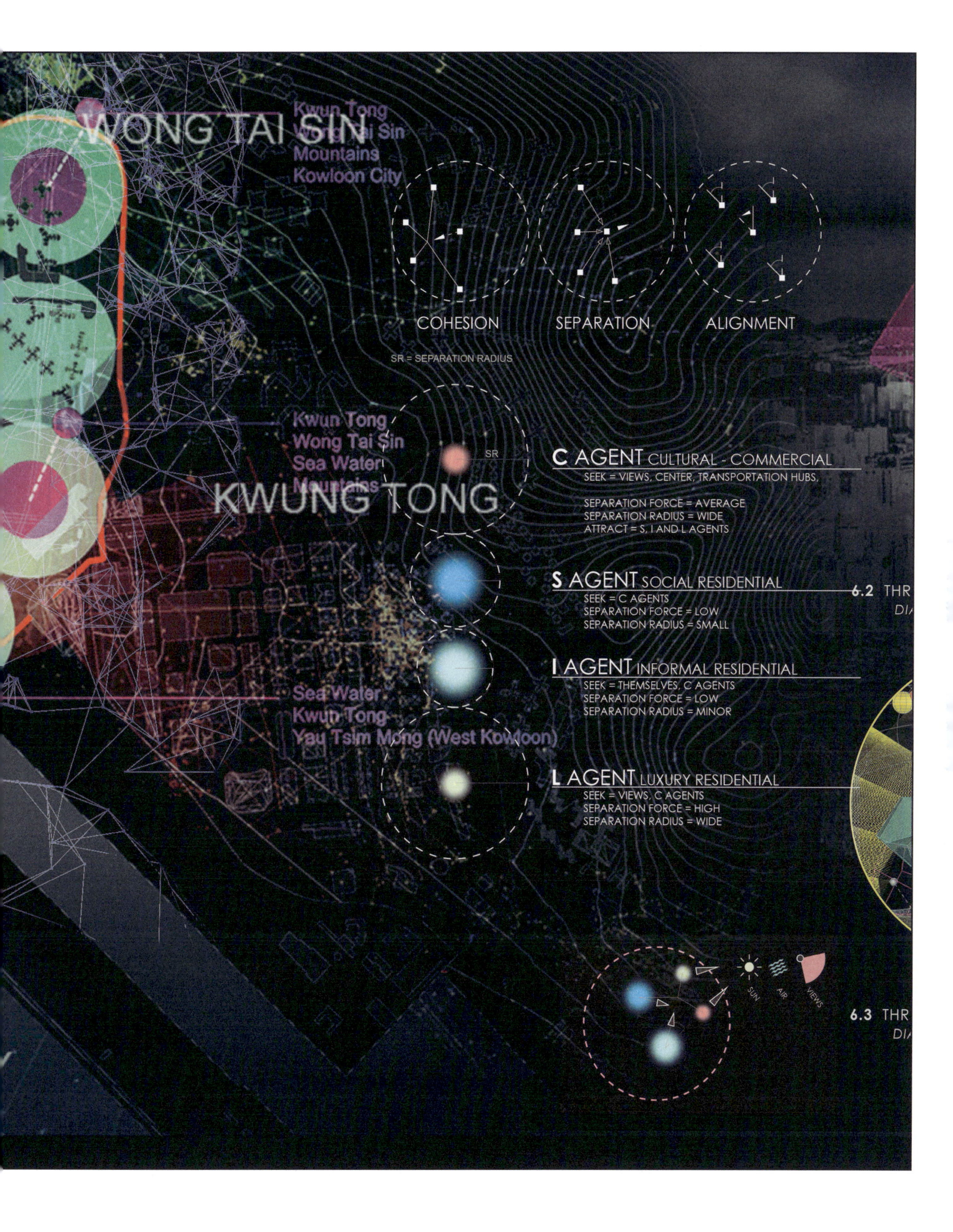
WONG TAI SIN
Kwun Tong
Wong Tai Sin
Mountains
Kowloon City
COHESION
SEPARATION
ALIGNMENT
SR = SEPARATION RADIUS
Kwun Tong
Wong Tai Sin
Sea Water
Mountains
KWUNG TONG
SR
C AGENT CULTURAL - COMMERCIAL
SEEK = VIEWS, CENTER, TRANSPORTATION HUBS,
SEPARATION FORCE = AVERAGE
SEPARATION RADIUS = WIDE
ATTRACT = S, I AND L AGENTS
S AGENT SOCIAL RESIDENTIAL
SEEK = C AGENTS
SEPARATION FORCE = LOW
SEPARATION RADIUS = SMALL
I AGENT INFORMAL RESIDENTIAL
SEEK = THEMSELVES, C AGENTS
SEPARATION FORCE = LOW
SEPARATION RADIUS = MINOR
L AGENT LUXURY RESIDENTIAL
SEEK = VIEWS, C AGENTS
SEPARATION FORCE = HIGH
SEPARATION RADIUS = WIDE
Sea Water
Kwun Tong
Yau Tsim Mong (West Kowloon)
SUN
AIR
VIEWS
6.2 THR
6.3 THR

three-dimensional city plot distribution

HIGH DENSITY CELLS
CITY CENTERS
6.4 THREE-DIMENSIONAL PLOTS
TOP VIEW
CV
INDEX + REFERENCES

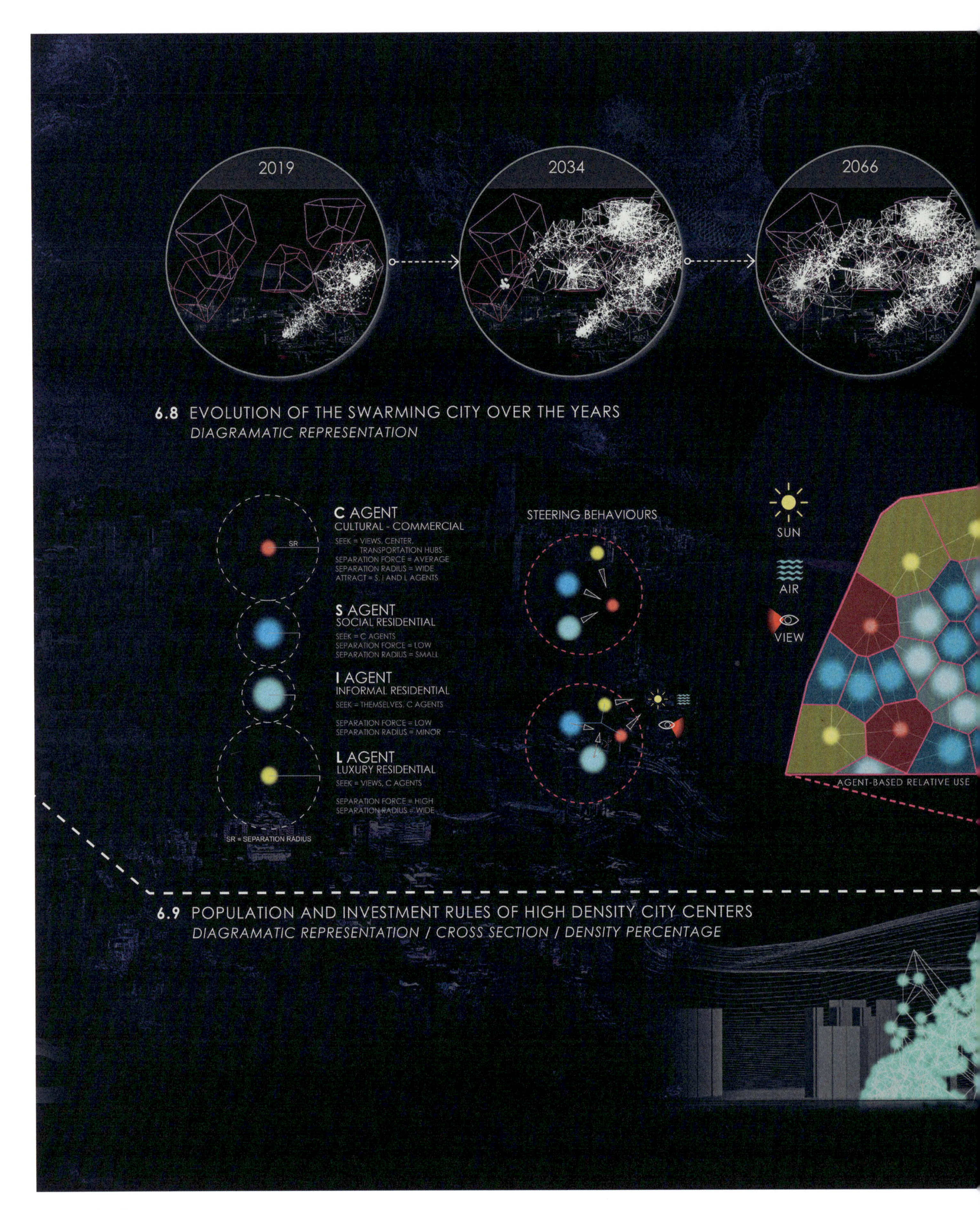

city growth rules over time

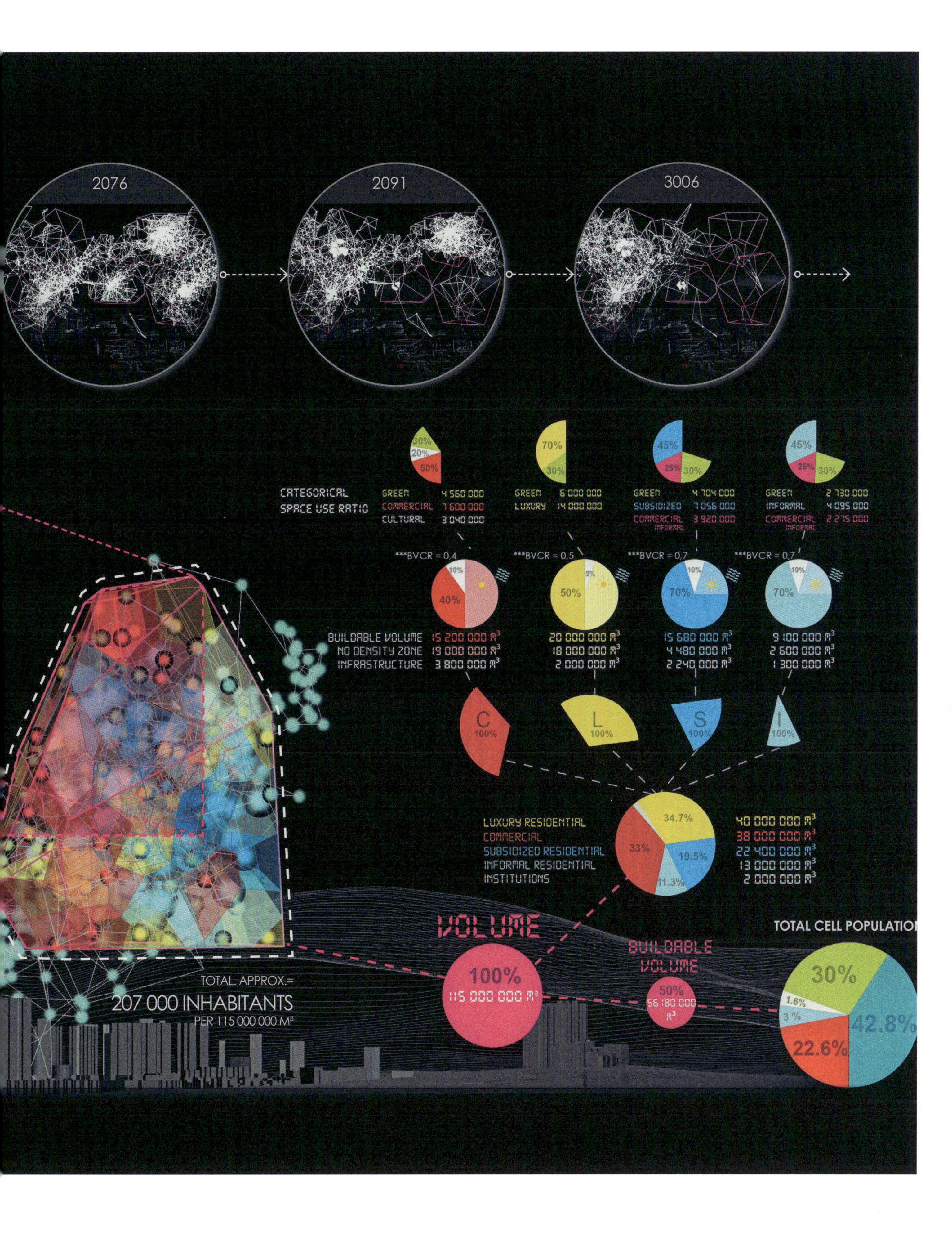
2076
2091
3006
30%
20%
50%
70%
30%
45%
25%
30%
45%
25%
30%
CATEGORICAL
SPACE USE RATIO
GREEN 4 560 000
COMMERCIAL 7 600 000
CULTURAL 3 040 000
GREEN 6 000 000
LUXURY 14 000 000
GREEN 4 704 000
SUBSIDIZED 7 056 000
COMMERCIAL 3 920 000
GREEN 2 730 000
INFORMAL 4 095 000
COMMERCIAL 2 275 000
***BVCR = 0,4
***BVCR = 0,5
***BVCR = 0,7
***BVCR = 0,7
10%
40%
5%
50%
10%
70%
10%
70%
BUILDABLE VOLUME 15 200 000 M³
NO DENSITY ZONE 19 000 000 M³
INFRASTRUCTURE 3 800 000 M³
20 000 000 M³
18 000 000 M³
2 000 000 M³
15 680 000 M³
4 480 000 M³
2 240 000 M³
9 100 000 M³
2 600 000 M³
1 300 000 M³
C 100%
L 100%
S 100%
I 100%
LUXURY RESIDENTIAL
COMMERCIAL
SUBSIDIZED RESIDENTIAL
INFORMAL RESIDENTIAL
INSTITUTIONS
34.7%
33%
19.5%
11.3%
40 000 000 M³
38 000 000 M³
22 400 000 M³
13 000 000 M³
2 000 000 M³
VOLUME
100%
115 000 000 M³
BUILDABLE VOLUME
50%
56 180 000 M³
TOTAL CELL POPULATIO
30%
1.6%
3 %
42.8%
22.6%
TOTAL APPROX.=
207 000 INHABITANTS
PER 115 000 000 M³

city growth over one decade

1
2
3
7
8

4
5
6
9
10

Credits

Entering the Universe of Possibilities
Image Credits: Xuan Xie, Jessica Seipp

Studio Instructors: Frank Stepper, Timo Carl, Vanja Juric

Studio Tutors: Tina Heidenreich, Sarah Metwally, Eugenia Schlag, Patrick Euler, Niklas Rieckmann

FEATURED PROJECTS

Radhäuser 2019, Kassel, Germany

Project Bike Carousel: Axel Lippram; David Sadowsky
Image and Video Credits: Axel Lippram; David Sadowsky

Park Der (T)Räume 2015, Paris, France

Project Magnetic Space: Sarah Metwally, Eugenia Schlag
Image and Video Credits: Sarah Metwally, Eugenia Schlag

Experiment in Architecture, Thinking the Impossible
Image Credits: Xuan Xie, Julian Fiegehenn

Studio Instructors: Frank Stepper, Timo Carl

FEATURED PROJECTS

Vertical City 2018, Vienna, Austria
Image Credit: Julian Fiegehenn, Philipp Pusceddu

Project Jupiter Clouds: Julian Fiegehenn, Philipp Pusceddu
Image and Video Credits: Julian Fiegehenn, Philipp Pusceddu

Project Vertical Wave: Ran Li, Yunjie Chung
Image and Video Credits: Ran Li, Yunjie Chung

Berlin Tegel Airport 2012, Germany
Image Credit: Ernesto M. Mulch, Stefan Niggemeyer

Project Flyscraper: Ernesto M. Mulch, Stefan Niggemeyer
Image and Video Credits: Ernesto M. Mulch, Stefan Niggemeyer

Land Unter 2016, Madjuro, Marshall Islands
Image Credit: Elena Mateev

Project Elastic Space: Zhikai Feng
Image and Video Credits: Zhikai Feng

Project Deep Growth: Elena Mateev
Image and Video Credits: Elena Mateev

Guggenheim Helsinki 2014, Finland
Image Credit: Andreas Göbert, Patrick Euler

Project Synthesystem: Andreas Göbert, Patrick Euler
Image and Video Credits: Andreas Göbert, Patrick Euler

Experimenting with Real World Parameters
Image Credits: Timo Carl

FEATURED PROJECTS

Solar Spline 2017, Kassel, Germany

Seminar Instructors: Timo Carl, Markus Schein, Frank Stepper

Student Team: Wassim Daaboul, Mahmoud Dames, Grischa Göbel, Annemarie Kroworsch, Elena Mateev, Ahmed Teftafeh,Tuantai Truong, Bastian Wiesel

Image Credits: Timo Carl, Markus Schein, Flying Impressions

Free Skin 2015, Kassel, Germany

Seminar Instructors: Timo Carl, Vanja Juric, Frank Stepper, Mathias Käbisch

Tutors: Grischa Göbel, Bastian Wiesel

Student Team: Line Umbach, Tim Stöhr, Eric Wiederhold, Lena Henriette Neuber, Anne Liebringshausen, Oliver Raderschall, Philipp Kern, Jonathan Schmidt, Christian Slama, Cagdas Alakus

Image Credits: Timo Carl and above students

Urban Glow 2013, Kassel, Germany

Seminar Instructors: Timo Carl, Vanja Juric, Frank Stepper, Olaf Val

Student Team: Jan Houdek, Frederick Ecke, Fabian Friedrich, Eleonore Feser, Ina Petri, Abbasian Sharam, Metz Sarah, Jasper Meiners, Isabel Paehr, Patrick Euler, Michael Kraft

Image Credits: Timo Carl and above students

Lost And Found 2020

Seminar Instructors: Sarah Blahut and Frank Stepper

Student work: Wenyu Jia

In Search of Free Space in the Design Process
Image Credits: Xuan Xie, Ricardo Valencia Paéz

MA and BA Thesis Advisors: Frank Stepper, Timo Carl

FEATURED PROJECTS MASTER

Roda (Re)ação 2012, Rio de Janeiro, Brazil

Project Credits: Ernesto M. Mulch, Stefan Niggemeyer
Image Credits: Ernesto M. Mulch, Stefan Niggemeyer

Kowloon Walled City 2013, Hong Kong, China

Project Credits: Ricardo Valencia Paéz
Image Credits: Ricardo Valencia Paéz

FEATURED PROJECTS BACHELOR

Explosionsräume 2018, Anywhere

Project Credits: Sarah Metwally, Eugenia Schlag
Image Credits: Sarah Metwally, Eugenia Schlag

Excursions

INSPIRATIONS FROM VENICE 2014

Patrick Euler, Harun Faizi, Cynthia Ward, Jonas Eichinger, Brigitte Osenstädter, Felix Lehr, Jule Engelhardt, Oliver Waldsachs, Mariam Shubbak, Edwin Koch, Han Feng, Sina Danneberg, Laura Heimann, Rita Bogdantschnik, Angelina Grubert, Jennifer Neuschäfer, Lucas Hundt, Alexander Pfeifer, Dacic Rukija, Sarah Metwally, Susanne Becker, Eugenia Schlag, Amet Soytek, Julia Pötter

Image Credits: Frank Stepper, Timo Carl, and above students

INSPIRATIONS FROM COPENHAGEN, DENMARK 2016

Evelyn Klein, Alicia Dobrinski, Florian Heiß, Anna-Lena Schmitz, Manuel Walter Cichos, Qinwen Jia, Wenju Jia, Annabell Nehrlich, Jessica Brcelic, Beatrix Meisner, Philipp Erdman, Soner Gökhan Yildiz, Alexandra Zhukov, Michelle Albrecht, Eric Schmidt, Felix Breitenstein, Leon Frohnert, Christin Schäfer, Alina Morkel, Laura Goldmann, Sammuel Fellmann, Kimberly Kues, Sarah Shakir, Tabea Schwaneberg, Melisa Bastimur

Image Credits: Frank Stepper, Timo Carl, and above students

INSPIRATIONS FROM FRANCE 2015, 2017

Zahedeh Pourkarimi, Mahtab Mounesan, Sarah Metwally, Kimberley Kues, Alina Morkel, Tina Haidenreich, Jessica Henkel, Eric Schmidt, Christin Schäfer, Christine Marx, Maik Kleiner, Alina Riebel, Dowe Larissa, Linus Netzband, Maik Lotz, Tabea Bühler, Anna-Karina Leathers, Jérémy Leclercq, Rico Pfleger, Qi Hu, Ke Shi, Jule Engelhardt, Alexander Pfeifer, Danneberg, Sina, Waldsachs, Oliver, Han Feng, Edwin Koch, Felix Eric Lehr, Lucas Hundt, Angelina Grubert, Julian Stepper

Image Credits: Frank Stepper, Timo Carl, and above students

INSPIRATIONS FROM LOS ANGELES, USA 2013

Julian Fiegehenn, Philipp Pusceddu, Adrian Bochynek, Jonas Eichinger, Sarah Steinhäusser, Christian Slama, Julia Kohlbek, Daniela Friedewald, Oliver Raderschall, Line Umbach, Johannes Schürmann, Stefan Niggemeyer, Sarah Metz, Vanja Juric

Image Credits: Frank Stepper, Timo Carl, and above students

Short Bio Editors

Frank Stepper was born in 1955 in Stuttgart. He was educated at the University of Stuttgart and at the Technical University of Vienna and received his diploma degree in architecture at the University of Stuttgart in 1984. From 1985 until 1988 Frank Stepper worked with Behnisch & Partners, Stuttgart, as Project Architect responsible for the prize winning Hysolar project at the campus of the University of Stuttgart. In 1988 he joined Coop Himmelb(l)au, opening and managing the Los Angeles office, where in 1990 he became a Partner with Coop Himmelb(l)au, Vienna.

From 1989 to 1995 Frank Stepper was a Studio Instructor and Thesis Advisor at the Southern California Institute of Architecture (SCI-Arc) in Los Angeles. From 1998 to 1999 he was Visiting Professor at the University of Kassel, where he was made Professor for Design and Technology at the Department of Architecture in 2000 and continues to teach. Since 1988 Frank Stepper has been a member of the Architectural Association of Germany.

Timo Carl is an architect and Professor for Digital Design and Construction at the Frankfurt University of Applied Sciences, where he co-leads the interdisciplinary research group ReSULT (Research into Lightweight and Sustainable Building Technologies). His research interests include the aesthetics of progressive technologies and computational design methods within the field of architecture. Until 2019, he taught experimental design at the University of Kassel, where he completed his PhD thesis and received multiple awards for his work.

Sarah Blahut is a Berlin-based architect with more than 15 years of international experience working on notable and prize winning projects in Los Angeles, London, Berlin, and Leipzig. She holds a Bachelor of Arts in Architectural Studies from the University of Kansas and a Master of Architecture from the Southern California Institute of Architecture. Since 2019, Sarah has been teaching design studios and seminars at the University of Kassel, where she is also a PhD candidate researching experimental design with augmented and mixed reality systems in architectural representation.

Imprint

Editors: Frank Stepper, Timo Carl, Sarah Blahut
Concept: Frank Stepper, Timo Carl, Sarah Blahut, and EEK Students

Acquisitions Editor: Alexander Felix, Birkhäuser Verlag, CHE-Basel
Content Editor: Angelika Gaal, Birkhäuser Verlag, AUT-Vienna
Production Editor: Anja Haering, Birkhäuser Verlag, GER-Berlin
Translation from German into English: Sarah Blahut, GER-Berlin
Copyediting: Word Up!, USA-Missoula
Layout, cover design, and typography: typoint, GER-Berlin
Image editing: LVD Gesellschaft für Datenverarbeitung mbH, GER-Berlin
Printing: Beltz Grafische Betriebe GmbH, GER-Bad Langensalza

Typeface: Miller, Soleil

Library of Congress Control Number: 2023932941

Bibliographic information published by the German National Library
The German National Library lists this publication in the Deutsche Nationalbibliografie; detailed bibliographic data are available on the Internet at http://dnb.dnb.de.

ISBN 978-3-0356-2622-3
e-ISBN (PDF) 978-3-0356-2627-8

P. O. Box 44, 4009 Basel, Switzerland
Part of Walter de Gruyter GmbH, Berlin / Boston

9 8 7 6 5 4 3 2 1 www.birkhauser.com